Twelve Mile Prairie

*To Vincent Barry
Love y'a Dad*

Royd Wayne Newton

Twelve Mile Prairie

Loyd Wayne Newton

iUniverse, Inc.
New York Bloomington Shanghai

Twelve Mile Prairie

Copyright © 2008 by Loyd W. Newton

All rights reserved. No part of this book may be used or reproduced by any means, graphic, electronic, or mechanical, including photocopying, recording, taping or by any information storage retrieval system without the written permission of the publisher except in the case of brief quotations embodied in critical articles and reviews.

iUniverse books may be ordered through booksellers or by contacting:

iUniverse
1663 Liberty Drive
Bloomington, IN 47403
www.iuniverse.com
1-800-Authors (1-800-288-4677)

Because of the dynamic nature of the Internet, any Web addresses or links contained in this book may have changed since publication and may no longer be valid.

The views expressed in this work are solely those of the author and do not necessarily reflect the views of the publisher, and the publisher hereby disclaims any responsibility for them.

ISBN: 978-0-595-48672-4 (pbk)
ISBN: 978-0-595-61105-8 (cloth)
ISBN: 978-0-595-60767-9 (ebk)

Printed in the United States of America

Contents

Preface vii
Acknowledgments ix
Poem "Twelve Mile Prairie" xi
Introduction xiii
Chapter 1: Mecklenburg County Virginia/Indian
            Territory/George 1
Chapter 2: Indian Territory/Statehood/William and Della 11
Chapter 3: Lloyd and Thelma 30
Chapter 4: My Experience 43
Chapter 5: Our Legacy 63
Chapter 6: Generations 68
Chapter 7: Reminiscences, Poetry and Songs 127
Conclusion 155
References 157

Preface

The history and origin of Twelve Mile Prairie of Indian Territory has started my quest for this heritage to be exposed. My Great Grandfather Newton and his descendants, the human beings that shaped the course of this past, and why he chose to settle a remote place is the one reason to enjoy this history. This is a true collaboration of efforts. It was this legacy and passion for generations that actually spawned my attempt to pursue the ancestry and uncover nature's dialogue. The question is what would life for me be like born in another scenario like New York City or the west coast or somewhere besides this prairie?

Now in my life long approximation, destiny made its' claim on my life. Ultimately the ball is in my court. I have lived these legacies to share it with all of my family and descendants and friends. This is an heirloom for generations to come.

It is my pleasure to have the opportunity to share the ancestry and family experiences along with numerous conversations and correspondence with relatives, acquaintances, and friends whose input made it possible for these authentic accounts.

L.W.N

Acknowledgments

My gratitude to Susan Driscoll and Diane Gedymin for their phenomenal efforts and all the support of everyone at IUniverse. Special thanks to Collin County Living Civil War Historians, Dennis Todd, and Rodney Stell for the Civil War re-enactment and encouragements.

Thanks to my wife Becky, Boyd Newton, BB Newton, Jimmy Newton, my daughters Tracy, Christie, and April and my sisters Janell, Dreatha, Linda, and Sharon Elaine for all the support.

Thanks for all the memories of Twelve Mile Prairie by Walter Smith, Janell Newton Adams, Shirley Studdard Ross, Pasty Allen Sharbutt, Betty Newton Young, Barbara Newton Kendrick, and Randy Adams. Thanks for the songs written by Linda Kay Newton Holland, Boyd Lynn Newton, and Lola Newton.

Thanks for the poems written by B.B. Newton. Special thanks to Boyd Newton, B.B. Newton, Brenda Gardner Weatherbee, Betty Newton Young, Jean Newton Hall, Louie Newton, Barbara Newton Kendrick, Maylene Newton Claborn, Harold (Harry) Newton, Gladine Pace Newton, Herschel and Jewel Justus, Betty Justus Donaldson, Bonnie Justus Goss, Charlotte Lyday and every person that assisted with the genealogy of Chapter Six.

Twelve Mile Prairie

Upon this Land, that truly God has made was placed a Family rooted and grounded with His Grace!

From the Prairie to the Streams and the Lakes, it was Elohem!

From the Beginning till the End in my Memories, I will always think of Him!

From the Dawn of every New Day let Me always Come & Pray!

Giving Him Thanks to let Me Stay!

Loyd Wayne Newton

Introduction

This book was written in relation to the direct decedents of the Newton's of Mecklenburg County, Virginia which was formed in 1764. James Newton, the father of my Great Grandfather, George Washington Newton, along with his brother, John, all fought in the Civil War.

They fought in the 38th regiment of the Virginia Infantry organized in Pittsylvania County, Virginia in June of 1861. They served under the command of Generals Early, Garland, Armistead, Barton and Stewart. My great grandfather, George Washington Newton joined company "D" of the 38th regiment on May 3, 1861, as a private with "Whitmell Guards."

The Governor of Virginia, John Letcher called for the men of Virginia to leave their families and occupations and join the Confederate Army. The 38th consisted of ten companies most of which were organized in Pittsylavania County, Virginia. Captain Ralph Herndon was the initial leader of Company D.

The engagements and assignments of the 38th began May 5, 1862, with the battle of Williamsburg, and continued at the battle of Seven Pines where the 38th suffers a casualty rate of 42 percent. Then on July 1, 1862, the third battle was at Malvern Hill, where they suffered severely with eleven killed, 72 wounded and eleven missing. In September 15, 1862 they took part in capturing Harper's Ferry. In September 16, 1862, they joined the battle of Sharpsburg. They took up battle again on July 3, 1863, where they fought in Pickett's charge at Gettysburg where Colonel Edmonds died and of the 481 members of the 38th, 40 were killed on the battlefield, 51 wounded and 103 captured.

Then on May 10, 1864, at the battle of Chester Station, Colonel Cabell was killed. Soon thereafter, the regiment continued to fight at Drewry's Bluff on May 16, 1864, where 23 were killed and 77 wounded. It was November 17, 1864, that the 38th captured the Union line near Petersburg. Then on April 1, 1865, they fought at the battle of Five Forks. The battle of Sayler's Creek was the final battle of the 38th regiment on April 6, 1865. It was April 9, 1865 at Appomattox that General Lee surrendered in the courthouse and just two miles away at Pleasant Retreat, the 38th were waiting. The 38th broke camp on April 13, 1865, and headed home.

After the war, George Washington Newton married Althea Crumply and moved to Mississippi where she bore him a son, William Edward. William was four years old when his mother, Althea, died from childbirth. After Althea died, George left William with friends in Mississippi, as they were the only ones he trusted until he could find his own place.

George traveled back home to be with his Dad in Virginia, and shortly afterwards went to Indian Territory and became preoccupied with the prairie that he named, Twelve Mile Prairie. George built a home on the twelve mile prairie and went back to Mississippi to get his son. The friends entrusted with William wanted to move to Dallas, Texas. George and William helped their friends move to Dallas and in the process stayed for awhile and started a produce farm where they sold vegetables to Dallas residents.

It was in Dallas where William met Della Penny and later they married in Sherman, Texas. After they were married, they moved to Indian Territory in an area that later became Bryan County when Oklahoma on November 16, 1907, became the 46th state of the United States of America. Bryan County became known as the Choctaw Nation of Oklahoma.

Fourteen children were born to William and Della but only twelve survived to adulthood. George Washington Newton lived on the prairie until his health began to fail him. Subsequently, he moved to a Confederate home in Ardmore, Oklahoma and lived there until his death. William and Della lived all their life on the prairie leaving the legacy to their sons George, Floyd, Lloyd and Boyd. George moved to Bakersfield, California and Floyd moved there a few years later.

Lloyd, Boyd, and Zora continued to live on the home place with the responsibility of the estate. Boyd eventually moved to his own place just one mile north of the Newton estate. Lloyd and Zora continued working the original property. When Zora passed away, her sister, Marie, inherited her portion of the land which she later bequeathed to her own daughter, Brenda. When Lloyd died, his son's, Loyd Wayne and Jimmy Harold, and daughters Janell, Dretha, Linda Kaye, and Sharon Elaine inherited his part of the estate. Jimmy Newton and his son Timmy Newton and the daughter of Boyd Newton, Lola Newton Gresham, all still own portions of the Newton estate on Twelve Mile Prairie.

Chapter 1

Mecklenburg County Virginia/Indian Territory/George

1845/1899

It was before statehood and returning from the Civil War, I, George Washington Newton, walked upon this wild frontier. A small creek flowed there in the wilderness upon a ridge between the willow saplings. Suddenly, there appeared a mysterious Indian, sitting upon a paint horse, with a heart of a deer in his hand, watching from afar. This grassland paradise stretched as far as the eye could conceive as timber only grew along the creek bottoms and streams. This land was covered with lush tall grass in virgin perspective.

It was then that I made my claim upon this land. I felt my destiny approaching like a lighting bolt from the sky, telling me that this is the place I should be. Moving from the state of Virginia, and leaving it all behind had been a challenge from the start.

I looked upon the excess of the land and envisioned fields of cotton, corn, peanut, wheat, oats and tobacco, which enhanced the feelings of home. It's that vision that compelled the outcome of my hopes and dreams for years to come for this prairie. The movement of the native grass, which grew so prevalent, was breathtaking to see, as was the beauty of this meadowed land. I was infatuated and empowered not only by this beauty, but also by the freshness and untouched purity of the scene before me.

The whole idea began to exhaust me knowing the work that lay ahead. Preparing for the necessary steps became my focus. I was willing to take on the challenge as I remembered that one day during the war, I had told myself that if fortunate enough to make it out alive, I would find a place for myself and lay down roots.

My father, James, kept telling me to go west for that is the future. I listened, and I asked my brother, John, to come along with me. I remembered the words that transpired between us. "Why don't you come with me, John?" I had said. After a minute he said, "Why?" "Because of the opportunities there would be for you," I said. "Opportunity! Is that it," he said. "Yes! Why not, John? What's there ever going to be for you here?" He replied, "Just family, people I love, and a good home." "Have it your way," I said, "but don't say I didn't give you a chance to come with me."

After the conversation he still insisted that his place was there in Virginia with Dad. Perhaps he felt this way because they had both fought in the same company in the war; and that Dad had always looked after him since he was the youngest. I knew they both had enough of the adventurer's blood in them to understand why I had to go. Who could tell how long it would be until I would see them again, if ever.

I stopped to set up camp and begin planning for my new home. After supper, alone in the night, I began to remember my joining Company D of the 38th Regiment that was organized in Pittsylvania County in Virginia, in June of 1861. I served under the command of General Early, Captain Herndon, and Captain Baggett as we fought from Williamsburg to Gettysburg. It seemed that thoughts of the war were with me constantly.

James, a friend of mine, was a corporal in our company and another boy we met John, was a private, like myself. We three bonded so easily with the other troops in our loyalty to the Confederacy, and fought for our lives at Drewry's Bluff and Cold Harbor. Then later we endured the hardships of the Petersburg trenches, Chester Station, Five Forks, and the finality of the war at Appomattox.

I'll always remember a quote from General Lee, "I have fought against the people of the North because I believed they were seeking to wrest from the South its dearest rights. But I have never seen a day when I did not pray for them." This sealed my conscience belief of the sincerity of the Confederates. Even the very name Robert E. Lee struck fear into the hearts of loyal northerners. I went to bed that first night and dreamt of my new life.

Born December 28, 1845, Mecklenburg County, Virginia was home then, but now it was this prairie that had a spell over me. On this land were angry Indians who were upset at having to share their territory with the newcomers. Not far away the U.S. Army had built Fort Washita, under the instructions of "old rough and ready" Zachary Taylor, who afterwards became the president of the United States. Before the Civil War, the fort was well manned with cavalry troops, and then seized by the Confederacy in 1861 and remained garrisoned until 1865.

During the Civil War, individual Indians were divided between loyalty to the Confederacy or neutrality; however, tribal governments officially sided with the South. The rivalry turned to violence as Confederate factions attacked those Indians favoring neutrality, and forced them to flee. In this era after Civil War, the United States confiscated portions of the Indian Territory, and began resettling other tribes such as the Cheyenne, Arapaho, Kiowa, and the Comanche.

As non-Indian expansion pressed westward, the Federal government decided to relocate the Indians whose homes stood in the way of progress. The Choctaw, also known as Chakchiuma Indians, were relocated to Indian Territory. They were the Indians living in this area I wanted to call home and fortunately, seemed to be a peaceful group. I began to think of how my family would feel about living so close to Indians. My wife would have been intrigued.

As I remembered Althea, I thought of when we were married in 1872, in Jackson Mississippi, it seemed thoughts of her were always recurring in my mind. I missed her, but because of her I can keep my dreams alive through our son, William, who was born on December 11, 1876.

I allowed myself to think back to the night I could have lost everything, back when William was four years old. Althea was pregnant and her labor started. The mid wife discovered the baby was breech and knew she couldn't deliver. I sent William for the doctor that was miles away. William told me he came upon a mountain lion close to the river. He thought the lion was going to attack him when suddenly; the lion turned and spotted a small fawn a short distance away. The lion sprang for the fawn allowing William to pass with no harm.

William came back with the doctor but he was unable to save Althea and the baby. My sweet wife was taken along with our dream of her coming with me to this blessed land. Knowing William had no mother and that I was the only family he had, was the determining factor to carry the dream for Althea, and for my son, to find us a new home.

Leaving William with friends back in Mississippi was one of the hardest things I have endured. It was difficult to have him stay behind, but I knew it was best considering the conditions present were not suitable for him. After arriving here,

I hired in as the overseer for a large ranch close to the Red River, while planning for my own place on the prairie. This wild and undeveloped land was lonely without him and every night the howling of the timber wolves and panthers, as well as other night sounds, could be heard for hours as I lay unable to rest. The only exception was the whippoorwills that put me to sleep with that continuous echo of their call; it seemed they were there for a reason but I didn't know why.

Every day was a fresh adventure with building and clearing the way for something new to put in its place. The visits of the Indians were an everyday occurrence and it was like they were keeping an eye on me. Sometimes, I would put on the uniform of the Confederate and it seemed to provide me comfort and a sense of survival. Each day brought me closer to completion, but it was the many struggles that reminded me of how long it was going to take. My thoughts are often of the War and how I survived and how there was a driving force compelling me and sometimes I felt walking with me.

There was talk of the coming of a railroad, and this brought about excitement and change on the prairie. If this happens, life as we now know it will never be the same; but no one wanted to stand in the way of progress. The railroad they wanted to put through was one of the best things for the future and for the country. It would bring a means for commerce and trade, which encouraged people to build homes, schools, and stores and a faster way of travel to the western territories.

Riders came across the land saying that movement of Indians, buffalo, and herds of wild horses were headed this way and this will be a continuous event because of the government changing location of the Indians to this territory. I knew that anything could happen with the Indians, as they were known to be unpredictable, and small bands of them filtered through the woods, dragging tepees, and bundles of buffalo hides.

It was getting colder and I continued to work on our home, hoping to get enough finished to live in it before winter. Every day presented an invasion of Indians passing through and though they didn't seem to harm anyone, knowing what they could do kept me uneasy. This frontier forced me to stretch my body and my mind alike to the limits of survival. The supplies were getting low and I decided to go over to Nails Crossing to pick up a few things to get me through the winter. When I got there a coach was coming through on its way to Texas. They pulled up to let some folks off to rest while the teams of horses were changed.

This was the Butterfield Overland Stage route that crossed the Blue River that flowed southward through this prairie. It was a way to get across the Blue River to

Kenfic, which was just up the trail from here. I crossed over the long wooden suspended bridge that spanned the two embankments and there stood a store and a barn with a saddle shed, a hayloft and stalls for some 30 horses. The floor of the barn was made of thick four-inch walnut beams and just to the right was a large smokehouse with a good aroma from the sides of hanging pork and beef.

A wagon lumbered past me pulled by two teams of horses, their heads bent low, straining their collars, their hooves digging for each foot of ground while the teamster urged them on with the crack of his whip. Listening to the creaks of the heavy wagon, I felt a cold wind that stung my face and all day a cold and misty rain kept falling from the leaden clouds overhead. To my right, I spotted them through the trees, half dozen men on horseback with their hats pulled low and their collars turned up against the wind. An audible whisper rose as the wind caressed rough bark and swept past tightly bunched limbs, the trees literally humming through adversity.

In this same area was Fort McCullouch that was active during the start of the war in, 1862, under the command of General Albert Pike to the Confederacy in the department of the Indian Territory. The strange thing was this prairie was positioned in the middle of two forts, Fort Washtia on the west and Fort McCullough on the east and twelve miles of prairie in between.

A new year was here and the government decided to open new lands for non-Indian settlements in the western part of this territory starting "land runs". Settlers came across going west and talk was that they came from Poland, Germany, and Ireland to stake their claims. Texas cattlemen started cattle drives through the plains, drovers recognized the land for grazing, and ranches continued to thrive because of need for beef in other parts of the country.

Finally a post office was built in Durant, some twelve miles away. To get the mail, a trip was necessary once a month, which was usually the day set aside to pick up supplies.

New things were discovered each time I visited Durant and this time it was the newspaper and more railroads, both of which actually got the town buzzing. Durant began to gain more white settlers who came looking for a new life and to raise their families. They wanted the bottomland and the valleys of the Blue, Boggy, and Washita Rivers that were so fertile and soon became the favored spots to start row crops.

I mailed a letter to William telling him that I would come soon and move him here, but I had no idea how long it would take. To undertake a trip like that would take a long time and I wanted to make the best of it so that I had time to get back before winter. Settlers were moving in all around me and having neighbors was a good thing especially when help was needed. I also liked the thought of having a friend to look after this place until I could get back. The determining factor was to go get my son, and in the back of my mind I kept thinking how good it was going to be to get settled. Soon it would be time to go for him. I couldn't believe that he was soon to be thirteen.

The trip was long and when I got there William was sick and we had to wait before he could travel. My best friend Chestnut and his wife, the folks that William was staying with, decided to move to Texas. William and I made the decision to take the route through Texas to see what this new place was like and to help our friends get settled. However, along the way the wagon broke down, and had to be repaired adding unwanted length to our trip as well as unexpected expenses.

During this long journey the lack of sleep caused more flashbacks and dreaming of the war that constantly reminded me of the horrors I had faced. The fight at Gettysburg was devastating and I persistently heard the Colonel say, "One Southerner can whip three Northerners." I know it was a mistake, this war; it created the devil in a man. It seemed that it was in me now and it was hard to put things in their proper places. All the fighting and hardships that I encountered during the war unrelentingly made it hard on me, especially in my mind; remembering the things that no man should have to endure.

The North appeared as the heartless aggressor of the motherland, an aggressor whose ironbound legions had neither decency nor chivalry. The skirmish began; I could hear the irregular snap-snap and I saw the shells exploding leaving small white clouds. This was followed by a gigantic cloud of thick black smoke. I heard the great shells shrieking as they passed. I saw the pride of the men in their pieces. I could hear the cry of the regiment charging and the audible range hastening of infantry shifting positions. Then the chilling Southern yells and infantry hollering you "blue bellies;" and the Union soldiers in return hollering back you "graybacks."

Gettysburg was the bloodiest battle of the whole war. The dead lay everywhere. How could I ever be the same again? Never had I encountered so many things to think about in such a short time. It was the hour of my darkest despair the crisis of this war. This fate that rest upon me now was it to make me stronger or would it turn me to evil? This misfortune was in reverse of goodness through weakness that turned my unexpected nature to sin strongly.

A huge dark cloud settled over my spirit, and I couldn't get out from under its oppression. I was too depressed in my own thoughts to be afraid. The fighting was fierce, and the smoke so thick that sometimes it was hard to tell our own comrades from the enemy. As much horror as I had seen, I always knew the worst was yet to come.

This time twenty or thirty men had been dragged back to a holding place. As Armistead led the spearhead of the Pickett's charge now waiting at the top with his huge battery of forces along with General Robert E. Lee that was observing from the opposite ridge behind Pickett. Colonel Edmonds was shot and immediately carried back to the rear where he died.

Occupied with loading and shooting, then reloading again, I fought to survive. The Union troops were advancing through the underbrush. Union bayonets were all around me, one stabbing a comrade to my left of me then turning to the right. It was hand to hand combat with a large group of the union line as they moved past me.

I found myself lifting the limbs of my closest comrade; he was unconscious and the blood that was spilling out of his body from the gaping wound seeped like an overflowing volcano. Now the blood was all over my own arms and chest and he started to belch blood from his mouth. It appeared the bullet passed all the way through his body and he was not yet dead. I studied him with a prophetic eye, knowing that the atrocities of this war may well have taken his life. Upon meeting him, he displayed a youthful, blazing pride but tender like temper; however, now he lay in my arms, a broken, wounded man. I took comfort in the fact that I knew he was fervent in his faith and had been loyal and unswerving in his devotion to the cause.

I carried him back to where I found a wagon. The bullets were slamming into the wagon, splintering wood as I lay him inside it. I look around and I could see the soldiers on the side of the ridge as the Confederates charged up the hill though we fought the enemy off. The Union line crept down toward us again and then one small detachment of Confederate troops actually broke through the Union line right near the clump of trees. On horseback, riding stiff and brave soon to be cut to pieces by Confederate fire. For a short time there was pandemonium. Union soldiers were falling back right towards us, with shouts and orders filling the air.

I was completely out of breath when someone took me by the hand and started pulling me to a clump of trees; I was silently thanking God, thanking Him for saving my life. I opened my eyes seeing an enormous wave of Confederate troops.

The day was filled with scalding heat and still the smoke from guns and the dust from thousands of humans and hoofed feet clung in the air like a vapor from the pits of hell, burning my eyes and choking my lungs and the smell of death was everywhere. Lowering my eyes to take in the view from my left I felt the blood that was caked on the sleeve of my uniform.

The Confederates, in our attempt, were certainly crippled but far from broken. General Lee rode with the Pickett corps who had made the charge. He told us he was proud of our efforts. As night fell on this July third it was a day none of us will ever forget and one that left me with poignant sadness. It was finally silent when the grey uniform immediately identified himself as a Confederate officer. "We're pulling out, men!" he called out. "All of you that can travel, the wagon will be coming through." "We surrendering, Captain?," asked one of the wounded. "No, we ain't surrendering!," he shouted back angrily. "We're just getting you men out of here and back to Virginia." After whoops and hollers sounded at the mention of our home state, but mostly it remained quiet. The captain turned and left as quickly as he came. The rising sun would do nothing to change the exhausted and disheartened.

All through the night, General Lee pulled the men together from scattered positions as the Confederate wagons began making their way toward the mountain before swinging south. The turning point of the war had come during 1863 at Gettysburg, which beat Lee's invasion of the North. As the year ended, it seemed impossible that the South could win. Still the Confederacy refused to yield. Both the horror and the peculiarity were as perplexing and contradictory as the war itself. As a survivor, this war was the most intense experience I had ever encountered. This war has kept me looking back but in reality one of the most peaceful places now is this battlefield of which the Confederacy faced their fiercest war. Would these memories ever fade? Would I ever stop dreaming of these atrocities I endured?

The arrival to Texas was long and slow with everything that belonged to me in that wagon, and that fact made it difficult to trust anyone. We finally reached Dallas and stopped for another repair on the wagon. Chestnut purchased a piece of land on the edge of Dallas and William and I helped him start a vegetable farm. We then sold vegetables door to door to homes in Dallas on dirt streets.

Dallas was beginning to grow with immigrants coming in and settling all around us, which brought about extra money, but the thoughts of the prairie, kept lingering in my mind and night after night the feeling was so strong that I knew it was time to move on. William was curious of his surroundings and most of the time seemed restless. He began to take walks in the evenings and that's when he met Della Penny. Della became quite fond of William and they both seemed smitten with one another. Della told us the story of how she walked all the way from Knoxville, Tennessee to Texas with her family and a one-horse cart that only the smallest children could ride on. Being that Della was older, she made the journey on foot.

William was so intrigued with Della, but felt out of place in Dallas. I asked William if he was ready to move on to the prairie. He said, "Yes, that's what Mom wanted," lowering his head with that sad look on his face. "You miss her don't you, William," I said. He turned and looked me right straight in the eye and said, "You know she never had a chance, God took her." We have to let the dream stay alive!" I looked at William and asked if he was planning to marry Della. He looked back at me with a stern look that he always gave me and said that he had already asked her and she wanted to get married in Sherman because her family was there.

We started for Sherman as it was on our way back to the prairie anyhow. As we left Dallas, Della was nervous and her emotions were intense and the closer we got to Sherman the more anxious she got. William wasn't looking too good either; I guess the thought of meeting Della's parents was occupying his thoughts.

He stopped talking and I said, "You know you have to ask for her hand in marriage?" He said, "Yes, and I just want to get it over with." My next thought was of Althea, if only she could be here to make this a little easier, I wouldn't feel so alone. The next morning we pulled our wagon up to Mr. John Penny's home. Della eagerly greeted them and introduced the family to us. Then Della told her family that she was marrying William and moving to the prairie. It was the next day that William married Della.

When we arrived at the Red River, the only way to cross it was on the Colbert's Ferry. We paid a fee to cross over into Indian Territory. We stopped for the night on the banks of the river and other families camped next to us. More travelers were stopping for the night, as well. At one point, I gave William a roll of money and he put it with the saddle bags and used it for a pillow. I distinctly remember one couple with a tiny feist dog that the woman was holding and with her was a rather large man, her husband, I assumed. He must have seen me give William the money. During the night, that hefty figure of a man grabbed William around the neck, arousing me quickly. I took out my gun and hit him on the side of his head and he fell over the banks and into the river. I told William that was a close call and to watch more closely for dishonest people.

We were in the direction of the prairie, where our home would bring us to realism. The trails were narrow and the wilderness unfriendly, but opportunity was awaiting us like silent moments waiting to explain their existence. The closer we got to the prairie brought about overwhelming excitement to everyone. Della kept asking where is this place that you're so eager to be apart of. I told her the mystery of how ones' nature erupts when his dreams become a reality and owning this land would become just that.

We awoke to a fog that was overpowering the view. We were close to the prairie now, but we couldn't see ahead for the haze. Then there were arbitrarily delineated little patches and slopes and a creek bottom. I wanted my companions to see the beauty of the flowing grass on this beautiful land I called Twelve Mile Prairie.

Slowly, we inched closer as we approached our new home; I got the same feeling as when I first stepped upon this prairie. "Look William, see its beauty," I exclaimed. All of us got out of the wagon, and gazed with astonishment. "See, its better than I could have ever explained!"

The next word spoken was from Della when she lovingly looked at William and said, "This is our home; let this be our final investment William." I was comforted then with the realization that my son's family would love this land as much as I.

All at once the skies turned darker and darker and the rain came in large sheets. The air was damp from the rain and at rare intervals, I caught a glimpse of the torn edges of clouds hurrying ahead of a wind that was yet unfelt. Then the hail started and the wind picked up and the trees around us started to bend and move back and forth. Della turned to William and said she was afraid. Then, just as suddenly as it began, the rain had entirely stopped, but the clouds remained dark and heavy hanging low over the distant hills.

I laughed and told Della, "This is the way of the prairie. You'll just have to get used to it!" She spoke and said, "That doesn't mean I have to like it." Later, she told William that she couldn't believe she was venturing into the wilderness to live among savages and endure hardship and privation. She went on to say that it seemed just a month ago, she was mixing and mingling with Dallas society accompanied by William and enjoying life. Now, she was skeptical of her new life that offered a modicum of adventure and opportunity.

Chapter 2

▼

Indian Territory/ Statehood/William and Della

It must have been the unusual ardor of my gaze that turned her cheeks and brought her eyes back from the outside. She turned, flashing me a startled glance that caused my pulse to leap anew. Her eyes widened and a flush spread slowly upward toward her auburn hair then her eyelids drooped, as if weighted by unwanted shyness. Never before had a woman's expression aroused me like that and brought me to realization. I stopped her and we talked in half-light floating along together half dreamily.

For a long time we talked, so completely in concord that for the most part our voices were low and our sentences so incomplete that we sounded incoherent and foolish. Reaching out to give her support, my hand slipped down over her arm like a caress, until her palm lay in mine. With her trembling hand, she pushed from me. I felt a deep contentment and trying to analyze, I felt a little hostile like armies were fighting inside me. The mood passed and the darkness forced me to give instant attention to the path.

The legacy continues with me, William Edward Newton married on October 12, 1896, in Sherman, Texas to Della R. Nancy Penny, born September 18, 1875, in Knoxville, Tennessee. Enchanted to be a part of the wild frontier and excited about starting a family, my feelings were indescribable. It offered rich land, ample for our limited agricultural needs and it swarmed with myriads of wild beasts, birds, and fish in this fertile creek bottom. We were living almost to ourselves and supremely self-sufficient.

Della was determined to keep the dream a success and she knew what it would take and always gave her support. I was fortunate to have a wife of this caliber, as she gave me strength and motivation; she had boundless energy and limitless vision. We moved to the prairie and into the new home that was simply built. It was a four-sided figure house, with a living room, dining room, kitchen and two bedrooms. There was also a porch on both the front and back and a wood-burning heater kept the house warm. There was also a wood-burning cook stove in the kitchen. Coal oil lamps were purchased and used in all the rooms.

I was eager to be a part of this new place and well educated in farming. I took on the responsibility of this prairie, starting a row crop of corn and other crops, such as wheat and oats. I bought livestock, starting with cows, hogs, and chickens, along with the horses that I had brought with me to start the year. I took a liking to the land that was so fertile and was now ready to prepare this new land for farming and raising cattle.

We left large areas of the native grass to flourish as it had for years before our arrival. We desired to leave those lovely meadows to preserve what had been there from the beginning of this prairie. The plentiful grass had the appearance of beautiful fields of gold and became valuable as a good source of food for the livestock during the long, cold winters. Bois d'Arc Creek bordered one side of the land and supplied water for the livestock, and the home. Della liked the creek and used it often.

One day, Della was down at the creek. She told me she was looking over to the east as the sunrays were filtering through the early morning trees and noticed the clouds were heavy, but not enough to cover the sky. She felt an over whelming feeling come over her. She looked back across the creek and on the other side were a group of Indians, on horseback. She explained to me how fear flooded her instantly. They were gazing at her at the same time she noticed them and disappeared in the trees. Later, she asked me if I thought they might have been Comanche. I told her that if they were Comanche, they were probably just passing through and probably meant her no harm. This experience enforced my instincts to the treachery at hand; some Indians were not to be trusted. I asked her to never go down to the creek alone again, just in case. I did not want to scare her, but I was frightened by what could have happened. In fact, the thought made my blood run cold.

I was not accustomed to this black land but found new ways of tilling it, mostly through trial and error, and I soon became very successful at the art. I still used the old customs for breaking up the land and setting the row for planting, the horse and plow, just like my father had before me. Working the land was hard, but rewarding because, I knew this land could sustain my family.

Just after breakfast, I harnessed the horses and reined them out to the field on cue, and the horses leaned in the harness and stepped thick-muscled legged across the field, moving at a slow but steady pace. The musky scent of the horses lingered in the warm prairie sun as the plow laid down the furrow through the field. Plowed for the first time, the newly turned earth smelled clean and sweet. I could see the sweat under the forelocks turning and white lather forming between the legs and their sides were heaving from the pulling of the plow. I knew we were getting deep enough when their nostrils begin to flare.

At the end of the day I took them to the barn to cool down and let them unwind; then, slowly rubbed them down. I got the stalls ready, fed them, and put them in the stall for the night. In the late night breeze, I smelled the dust and horse sweat that was on my clothes.

It was always nice after a hard day's work to come home to my wife. Tonight, I didn't want to be alone with my thoughts. Della entered the room carrying a pitcher. She said, "Would you like some cold milk?" I replied, "I would like that, yes." I held out a goblet and Della poured the milk then set the pitcher on the sideboard. Della said, "Is there anything else you need?" Della sat down by my chair. Taking out my knife from my pocket wiped it off and begin to eat with it as always. I looked up from my plate and asked her to stay and keep me company. When silence settled over the table, the plate was clean and the hunger was gone from my belly. Della threw me a quick smile and said she would finish the dishes.

Finally, getting to settle in the house it was late in the evening and we were sitting in the living room just before bedtime. Della was mending a sock that I had ripped and I told her the supper was good tonight. She replied, "Thank you. William, that was a good thing to say, but tell me how you feel." I turned and faced her and said, "I feel with my hands." She laughed and said, "Oh! William, do you always have to say that?" I looked over at her and she said, "William, I love you!"

After a few months Della was showing signs of a new-comer and in the middle of the new year of, 1897, our first son George Edward was born, delivered by Della's mother; giving both of us a greater sense of attachment to the land and home we now shared. Shortly after George was born Mr. John Penny, Della's father, along with Della's mother Mary Elizabeth, came to live with us permanently since her father was paralyzed and had to have a lot of care and her mother wanted to help Della with the baby. Della's father's condition varied mysteriously; on good days, with the aid of two sticks, he could be moved from the bed to the his chair, but on bad days, and they came more frequent now, he barely had enough strength to crawl out of bed, dress and get into his chair.

Along with the things Mary brought was the old cast-iron cookware handed down from generation to generation. Included in the set were the Dutch ovens, deep skillets and shallow cornbread pans. These were the tools for perfect fried chicken and the years of use lent greatly to the cookware's history and legacy. A good cast-iron skillet has a unique recipe of its own; its' seasoning that is perfected over time. The seasoning is what makes it black and textured. Funny how life leads us back to the family, if we let it. There's nothing in the world that beats good old-fashioned southern cooking, and Della was the best.

Father, on the other hand, was content with living on the prairie and enjoyed the hunting and fishing especially on the Washita River. Father had strength; you couldn't help but see that and admire it. To have done what he did, to have marched out into the world alone to make a place for himself! Yes, you had to admire such vigor and will. Father's determination, that I have; it's something my father passed on to me.

Della took on the responsibility of all of us and never complained; the task of the early women of the prairie never ended from sunrise to sunset. Della worked with chores including churning milk for butter, planting a garden, and canning, a continuous task needed to keep a stock of food for the home. Sometimes, Della and I argued about her father, a man that I had no patience for. One night, Della stood in the bedroom and looked towards me. She asked me to help her with her father. When I turned to face her, she took a step forward and then stopped. I could tell Della was stunned by the look I gave her and she said, "You are cold and hard, Will." "Yes, I know", I replied, as if to deride her for asking me to help. She said, "Supper is ready in an hour," and with that she walked out of the room and gave me a stiff look. There was a flash of irritation and feeling in this expression and I felt a tightening of my mouth. I continued to walk to the bedroom knowing Della was furious with me for resenting her father living with us. It was obvious who was hard to live with.

Having so many in the house was difficult; however, the nights alone with Della were always good. It was nice having Mary here with us to help Della with the baby and besides, Della enjoyed having her family around. Mary helped Della deliver another baby, this time it was a girl, Bertha Elizabeth, on June 15, 1899, and this was a good addition to the family. Bertha was our first girl and in time, was a helper for Della, something she welcomed. With each new face came more things to do, but nothing too big for Della.

Bertha started walking early and was eager to discover her surroundings. I continued to plow and break up land for the food for the livestock, the fields were larger now and the yields from the harvest began to pay off. Life was moving along nicely.

One morning, Della and I were out on the porch when she asked me to open the old hickory barrel that was sitting there. Saying she had some cooking to do, Della began rolling out dough for a peach cobbler while standing at the kitchen table. She started talking about the first time she met me and seemed to be lost in thought. It had been four years and two children later and I still remember that day. She told me how much more she felt for me than when we first met. We talked for quite awhile and the cobbler she was preparing was almost finished baking. Della took the cobbler out, walked over to the window and gazed out, telling me how the sun felt warm. Then she placed the cobbler on the windowsill to let it cool.

Life was good, I reached up and smoothed a lock of her hair back from her brow, where she had attempted to push it aside only to have it fall once again and aggravate her all over again. She said it is good getting attention from me and this made her feel content. I went back to work in the hayfield and worked until the light of day disappeared. Afterwards, I had to finish the chores by lantern light. I was constantly telling Della how a farmer depends on the land and the weather. We raise what we eat and keep warm with the wood out of our timber. This is the freedom and the independence that comes from owing your own land. As I walked from the barn to the house, I thought I heard Della call my name. She called, "Will." I could hear the exhaustion in her voice as she said, "Supper is ready." I turned and looked at her and said, "Is that all?" She seemed puzzled by the question, and then she frowned at me and said, "What more do you want, Will?" I immediately felt sorry for my sarcasm, not knowing why I am so harsh, so often, to such a good woman. I thought to myself how lucky I am to have a wife that is willing to put up with my moods.

In the half-light of eventide, she looked at me and said, "Will, is that a smile in your eyes." She took a step closer, moving out of the doorway and onto the porch. She knew me well and could read the change in my attitude. She seemed dazed and reached out and touched me saying, "Am I dreaming this?" I took her hand and gently pulled her toward me. "I had forgotten how very beautiful you are," I said. I then claimed her lips in a kiss that was as sweet in its gentleness as it was searing in its passion. Della said it had been months since I had kissed her like that. She dissolved against me happy and confused. I felt her heart was racing, and I imagined her mind was spinning. Then she whispered against my shirt, "I don't understand". I replied, feeling her confusion, "I am not certain that I do either."

Reaching up, I gripped Della by the waist and lifted her up from the ground. Just for a second, conscious of the slight thickening of her middle. Briefly, meeting the upward glance of her eyes. Suddenly, I wondered whether this child's eyes would be like hers. With some surprise, I realized this was the first time I thought of the baby growing in her womb as a living entity, separate and distinct yet forever a part of us.

We were expecting our third child and Della went into labor. Mary took her hand and started wiping rivers of sweat from Della's face. After eight hours of labor, Della seemed no closer to giving birth than when she had started. Mary sat in the rocking chair knitting and seemed unconcerned by the delay. She got up and began to wipe more sweat from her face. Della had another contraction. She groaned loudly, squeezing Mary's hand; she was gripping it tightly. I thought a birthing bed is no place for a man to be. I turned to leave the room and Della cried, "Will, don't leave. We're having a baby." I could see the pain in her face anew. It was just a few minutes and Mary was holding a squalling, slippery baby in her arms, another girl arrived on May 21, 1902, and we named her Zora May.

Della whispered to us that she could stand a generous measure of pampering about now. Mary knew just what she needed and gave her a dose of paregoric and in just an hour she was resting comfortably. Now Della was getting more help to run the household, and could eventually delegate more of the work to Mary and the girls. It would be nice for her to have more time to herself. For instance, Della liked to read. Sometimes it was during churning the milk to butter she would start reading and when something she was reading got fascinating, the churning hand would slow down almost to a stop but picked up the pace when it was less interesting. Yes, Della would love to have more time for reading.

As time moved on, the prairie seemed to grow on everyone and working the land just enlarged our view of what we could plant next. We experimented with different crops and tried to overcome the grasses that kept coming back year after year. I got the feeling that this was all work and no play and I knew it was time for a change. Hunting was plentiful; therefore, I lost myself in the woods and found a nice young buck and took aim. To my astonishment, I hit it and it came down fast. I waited for a few minutes and started walking closer to the deer. It was a nice four-point buck. I gutted it, removed the musk bags, and then brought it home to Della for processing.

I thought this is far better than what Father had in the war. He told me about the only thing they had was boiled duck and that he got so tired of eating duck, but on the other hand it was what kept him alive and he didn't complain. He just kept saying, "Have you ever eaten any boiled duck?"

Soon, Della was heavy with child again. She waddled to the chair next to Mary, and then carefully eased herself into it. She placed a hand on the large mound of her protruding stomach. Mary must have caught the movement, as she looked towards Della who was glancing sharply at her. Della began rhythmically snapping beans into the pan on her lap while she studied her mother. The baby was not due for another two months yet; but, babies didn't always come when they were due. A couple months later, Della delivered another girl Lora Mamie, in the early part of 1904. Delivering babies was trying for anyone; however, Mary was always there for Della, which was a good thing for us.

Having Mary around the house had not been a problem for me, not like having Della's father around. She was a pleasant woman who had a nice presence about her. I always will remember her wearing that long apron that covered the front of her dress, and her auburn hair would be twisted in a knot at the back of her head. Smiles were always lifting the corners of her mouth, but never erased the hollowed look of tiredness around her eyes. There was also always a tolerance of a mother's love in her voice. In her room, there was a single bed with iron posts and frame tucked along a sidewall. She also had a washstand with a basin, where she would immerse her hands and wash with a chunk of lye soap. She would rinse with a water pitcher that stood beneath the west facing window that gave the room some natural light and ventilation. A patchwork quilt blanketed her bed, creating a cheerful splash of color next to the cream yellow walls. A rag rug of muted hues lay on the floor next to the bed.

Shortly, the prairie was in full bloom and the smell of the fruit trees and all the blossoms from the flowers seemed to set the pace. Spring was the most pleasing time of the year. Della liked the spring. The work was on her mind, the need to plant the garden and food for winter, as she knew it would be here faster than she wanted it to be. She kept asking me when we were going to have that ground broke up for the garden because it needed our attention. I thought, "When I have time, woman. You just can't snap your fingers and expect it to be done." Women, you can't live with them and you can't live with out them. What is a man to do?

The year had a lot going for it and another child brought smiles to us all. Lora was a natural beauty for the times and Della and I were making more calls on our neighbors, showing her off. Other talk was usually about stories of the issues with the Indians and some dreaded panther whose wailing cry sounded like a scream from a frightened woman. Much of life on the frontier had superstitious overtones and countless common place occurrences studied for portent. The moon had its strong supernatural influences and signs that were observed and taken to heart to provide us with the knowledge of when and how to do our planting and when to expect other events, like rain and storms. Some of our superstitions came from the Indians who were here before us and taught on how to read the land and the skies.

Into another year, Della was enjoying the family, but could sense something was wrong, but not rightfully put her finger on it. All the children were healthy and she was getting excited about the New Year. I could tell that she seemed preoccupied and worried. I rationalized by asking if she was okay and she would reply yes, though not very convincingly. Finally, after awhile, she spoke and said, "It's Mother that I am worried about. She has complained several times about not felling well. Mother keeps saying things that arouse my suspicions that something is wrong with her." After another few weeks, Della came from her mother's room one day and said, "Mother just passed away," as she glanced back to the door from whence she had moments ago come. She said, "I must return to her room. I have no other choice." As she slowly walked towards the back porch and held on to the baluster, Della's tears began rushing from her eyes. She told me that she had never felt so alone. I took her hands, trying to give her comfort. It seemed that she was shocked by my loving gestures towards her. I realized that it had been months since I had showed her affection and this seemed to be the tendency of Newton men, an inability to show warmth. Looking over at Della, I said, "Your mother was a good woman and one woman I will never forget." Mary Elizabeth died on March 11, 1905, too young to die, as she was only forty-four years old. I told Della that she didn't deserve to die.

Together, we walked out onto the veranda. Della appeared to be lost in her grief and I did not know how to reach her. In my desperation, I picked up the Bible and began leafing through it, searching for a way, any way, to help my wife. I looked up from my reading and noticed the great swath of grasslands before me. This prairie was one of our best kept secrets ... all of us here on this land ... but, today, I wondered if bringing my wife and her family here was best for them. I guess blaming myself was a way to relieve the burden for Della.

The following day, Della rose early to get ready for the funeral and she nervously remarked, "This is one day that I wish I had never been born." At the cemetery, the rain blew stinging cold wet rivulets down her neck. The minister's voice penetrated with intensity. Della cried, "She can't be dead, she can't be.

That can't be Mother lying there, in that pine box. She loved me; she was my closest friend." My poor wife appeared to be so desperate with grief. Not knowing what to do, I grasped her by the arm firmly at the ministers closing words and directed her away from the grave. Della was pulling away from me, wanting to stay with her mother, but I urged her forward ... back to the wagon ... back to her life without her mother.

We started on our way home on the mudded road. I reined the horses and the wagon started to move. Della did not speak and I just listened to the wheels splashing in the mud. Some of the mud splattered on Della's dress. Looking out at the people still standing around the grave, I felt angry. Della was looking too and she clasped my hand. I felt chilled to the bone. The wagon wheel sank into the deep ruts of the clay mudded road.

As the days went by, Della exhibited a special interest in a very unusual event happening in town. Everyone was talking about President Theodore Roosevelt, who was coming through this area on April 05, 1905. He came and spoke at Caddo and Durant as he was going through to a wolf hunt at Frederick. Della had great respect for President Roosevelt and being an avid reader, knew quite a bit about his policies and programs. His speaking near our little town seemed to bring her a small piece of happiness, but it was short lived.

After the speech, we were traversing the wheel rutted road coming from town. The wild grasses had been beaten into the sod by all the traffic and the dirt itself churned into mud. Della and I were following behind a crowded wagon ahead of us that had bumped and bounced over the bad rut. We had to stop and Della got out. The mud-splattered wagon rolled. I moved in her estimation, with irritating slowness. I said, "Are you all right?" I crouched next to her. She nodded affirmative, and tried to push her self up, but her hands slipped in the mud. "I'll help", I said, just as she fell. Momentarily, I froze, then stooped and wrapped my arm around her, feeling the protruding of her belly. This seemed the distinctive roundness of a woman in the middle months of pregnancy. Carefully altering my hold, I lifted Della to her feet. She hung her head and refused to look at me. "Are you with child," I questioned her? Della doubled over and I knew instantly that she was in pain. The fall had started her labor and she was breaking out in a sweat. I picked her up and put her in the wagon. I stopped by a lady in town who assisted in births. This time, Della did not have her mother there and unfortunately, our baby was stillborn. We lost our baby boy. Della became extremely saddened and refused to speak to anyone.

Despondent over the loss of both her mother and the baby boy brought her a lot of pain. She missed her mother's company and the stimulating conservations they always had in the evenings. Another year had presented itself and no one wanted to talk about the pain Della was going through. It seemed pointless to say anything because she was just going to do what she wanted and there was just nothing to change her mind. With these females you just have to let it run its course.

Soon, Della was in the family way again and delivered a boy later in the year. She delivered a little boy we named Louie, but within hours after birth, he died. Della's entire world was centered on her children. Each living child had become that much more precious to her. She couldn't bear to be parted from them for even a day. I understood that and without thinking, I caught myself obsessing over the events that had just taken place. This time it was different for Della. The loss of the last two children changed her perspective about life and I knew that time is what she needed, and insisted that she take time for herself.

One day, I accompanied Della on a walk. While wading in a creek, we saw a break in the willow trees. An early mist swiveled near the banks of the creek and rolled silently onto the narrow road, hovering close to the ground like thin white smoke. The road that skirted the edge of the valley was planted with corn and the green of the cornstalks shimmered in the early morning sun. As Della bent over to tighten her shoelace, a pen fell out of her hair. Under its sagging weight, her hair tumbled free from its bun. Hastily, she scooped the pin and tried to anchor it back in place. It was hot there at the creek, with no whisper of a breeze, not even in the shade, and the sweat rolled down our clothes, clinging to our skin. The heat was stifling; and it was difficult to concentrate on anything. We laughed as we pretended the creek was cool and that it caused us to shiver. This walk had proved to be a fun time for us both and I wondered why I didn't spend more time with Della this way. We headed back down the path to home.

Today, the familiar path crowded with memories, memories of more carefree days, the days when Della and I had first met and began our lives together. The evening filtered through the leaves of the large elm protruding the entrance of the yard. The sunlight and the breeze gleamed the essence of the prairie.

On November 16, 1907, this prairie was no longer called Indian Territory; it became Oklahoma, the 46th state of the United States of America. We had secured Statehood and people of the prairie became citizens of Bryan County which was created from the lands of the Choctaw. This County became known as the Choctaw Nation of Oklahoma.

Seasonal favorites sparked the appetite; Thanksgiving became more special because of statehood and it was truly a time of thanksgiving, feasting, expressing gratitude, and a chance to slow down to gather friends and family around us, and savor the aroma of the turkey roasting in the oven. As the neighbor ladies were helping in the kitchen, I closed my eyes and listened to all the sounds entering my head. I remembered it was the Native Americans who taught us how to pound the corn they had harvested into course meal that they mixed with water. The smells from the kitchen had brought on this memory and I anticipated a great meal soon.

It wasn't long before the snow arrived and laid a pure white blanket over the countryside. I was short on firewood. I hitched up the old mule to the sled and dragged in a load from where I had spent almost a day cutting. I lifted the reins and ripped them across the mule's back. When I returned, Della came out and helped me load a few pieces from the sled. Opening the hearth door, I loaded a log on the fire and after a while began vigorously stirring the fire with the iron poker, sending up a shower of sparks and crumbling the hot, glowing embers. As I added another log from the wood box the snapping and crackling of the new flames pierced the silence. I noticed Della staring into the fire, as she watched the small tongues of flame dart over the glowing embers, slowly devouring the log.

Another year had passed and Della seemed some better, but with child again and that is when Stella was born. Therefore, we had another girl, but she was born with a birth defect. Stella's middle fingers on both hands were grown together and that concerned Della and the family. We all welcomed Stella to the family in 1908. As our family was getting larger, it meant more responsibilities for Della and with the older daughters became a great help that we appreciated.

The rains set in for a few days and that is when you could find Della rocking gently in her chair. Today, we sat and listened to the rain slowly falling and just after a few hours I looked and she had finally fallen asleep. I also liked the rains and would slowly gravitate to the easy chair and find myself enjoying this down time, as well. It wasn't often with all the children, that we had any time to ourselves.

The year was 1909, and Della was pregnant again. Della said this morning for the first time, her baby had moved inside her womb. Although it had made her feel giddy and sick, her heart had leaped because of the life thus asserting itself, giving her own life meaning and purpose. She said that she prayed it would be a boy who would grow up to be the sort of man like me, but whether boy or girl, she would love and cherish it just the same. Suddenly, feeling a moment of hopelessness, she sought comfort by taking out her silver locket and looking at the two pictures inside. One was of her mother the other of her father. The picture was small and dim, but it was enough to bring to mind her mother's face and features that were plain, but honest, with its kindly look and twisted smile. The longing and the hopelessness passed. She closed the locket and tucked it inside her dress. As her strength and courage returned, she sat up and began to think about the future again.

The months passed and she delivered Linnie Ruth, with more girls causing enthusiasm in the family. With the family growing so fast, Della never had time for anything but the chores and caring for the children, whose needs seemed to grow with each additional mouth to feed. Working every day in the fields to keep the crops producing, and to get the yields, the need to sustain the family was on my mind constantly.

Spring had really waved her magic wand over the green prairie and splatters of Indian paintbrushes with their reddish-yellow splotches of color straight from the flowing meadows spread. I knew that Della enjoyed walking in the deep green grass and young weeds. She loved this time of year and her spirits seemed to lift. Besides breaking the land and the garden, I became busy building fences to give livestock more freedom. The cows and horses had chopped the grass in the small pasture short and there were cow piles scattered over the pasture like big brown buttons. We cut Bois d'Arc post from timber on the land and I purchased staples and barbed wire that was wound on big wooden spools. The fence protected the yard of our home, the garden, and barn to keep out the varmints.

Father was getting older and his health began to fail him and he needed more care. With great sadness, he decided to move to Ardmore to a Confederate home where doctors and nurses could give him the medical attention he needed. I knew it was hard for him to leave this prairie; after all, it was his dream for so long. As we readied the wagon to take him to his new home, he solemnly looked over the fields one last time and I felt a rush of pain for him.

Della was expecting again and this time it was a boy we named Floyd Rufus, born on July 15, 1911. The family was thrilled over another son. Everyone spoiled Floyd, especially George. He loved taking the baby outside in the evenings to calm his colic.

Suddenly, one night while we were outside on the porch, we heard noises coming from the barn! There were shadows momentarily darkening the entrance to the barn. Our young mare was lying stretched out on her side sweating bullets. We approached slowly. George took over and knelt by the mare's head, stroking her gently. I said, "You're doing the right thing; try to settle her down a bit." The mare turned her head at George as if to thank him for being patient. I said, "You're doing a good job." George was appalled by the blood, the sac, and the dark, wrinkled and flailing creature emerging, but he took it in stride.

This was a perfect delivery and George and I just stood there staring at the big baby colt, his long legs seemed to have unfolded and now were twice as long. In the next stall, was our old grey mare, who stood intently stirring. Of all the observers, human and equine, the old mare had been the most agitated; she was pacing, whinnying, and snorting.

Her behavior made us wonder if perhaps her hormones had been activated by some mysterious motherhood scent; she had never had a foal of her own. "That poor mare," George said. "It's as if she thinks she's the one delivering the baby." "She wants her own baby," I said," "You can't blame her." George and I then welcomed the young foal to the farm.

George Edward, now fourteen, became very good with horses and started breaking them for everyone. George was a natural when it came to a horse; he was a whisperer. He found a black colt and started working him and his coat shined with fear and sweat. The horse that George rode everywhere was a high-quality horse and it stood a good sixteen hands. The term he used was "he would eat out of your hands." George had the touch. The magic moment is when a horse begins to trust a man, George would say. George liked to go show off his horse to everyone, especially to Dewey, one of his best friends. He dismounted quickly and looped his reins around a hitching rail. Dewey asked George what he would take for that horse. He hesitated and that's when he said, "For you, I would give the best deal." They decided on a price and George sold the horse. The next week I overheard some of the men talking about George's old horse and come to find out the horse was blind.

The year was 1914. A brilliant blue sky and bright sun made the day look warm, but the air was frigidly cold. A chilly wind out of the artic north swept across the prairie, blasting the intense cold air that sent the temperature plummeting. My legs were numb with the cold and I could barely stay in the saddle. I had gone to town for supplies and it was getting late in the evening. Seeing the farmhouse in the distance, the horse snorted impatiently at the slow pace and strained against the bit, its neck tautly arched by the curbing reins. The horse was eager and started a prancing gait. I gave the animal its head and let it run as he knew he was home and couldn't wait for the feeding he knew would follow. It was a good thing that I was home on this December 10, because Della started labor and I, with help of the girls, delivered another son, we named Lloyd. Della became disturbed when she notice Lloyd's hands had the same birth defect like his sister Stella, except that the layer of skin was thin and we separated them ourselves.

Floyd and Lloyd, the young boys in the house, became a handful and I could sense Della favored them and was not as strict about correcting and overlooked little things they were doing. The girls were getting older and as I studied Bertha, who was more woman than child, I reached the realization that she was maturing. Women were like flowers. Not all bloomed early. She decided it was time to start a life of her own and married William Perry Justus on September 5, 1915 and moved to Wapanucka, Oklahoma.

As if to replace one child as they were moving on, Della and I had another baby girl, Beulah Ester, who was born on April 30, 1917. Beulah received a supreme reception from the family as we enjoyed having the new addition. Della and I knew the family needed more space and now with all the new additions, we bought another one hundred sixty acres of this prairie in 1918, and built a new home on the north side of the road. Everyone liked the changes and the new surroundings; our family was finally achieving the goals set before us. We had just settled in when another baby girl was born and we named her Velia Lillian in 1920. Velia was a very beautiful and her eyes would light up when spoken to, just like her smile. Having mostly girls in the home was a joy for Della and conversation was always geared for the female, leaving the boys separated from the talk. Our first born girls were growing older and leaving us, this time Lora married Earnest Justus and moved to Atoka, Oklahoma and started a family.

The prairie was turning a profit and I began to put money in the bank and started buying more equipment to cultivate more of the land. I built a blacksmith shop to take care of all the equipment I purchased. Della said I was one of the best blacksmiths in the county. I enjoyed working with the hot pits to create and repair; and, I must say, I was pretty good at it.

Another two years had passed and George Edward was becoming a man. He married Eunice Brake and then enticed by the ramblings of railroad men from the West, he took his new wife to Bakersfield, California, hearing that it was appealing with good farming and plentiful oil. Into that same year another boy was born on March 15, 1922, and we named him Boyd Willie. Boyd received his nickname early; we called him "Dick". Dick, along with Floyd and Lloyd, kept the family amused by constantly annoying the girls.

The hours became longer and working the land seemed endless with more land to till; but each additional son made it better for the family as a whole. As our boys were growing older, they were each more help to me and our land. I secretly hoped that my sons loved this land as I did and I wondered if they would continue to work this place after I was gone. My father had passed his dream of the prairie on to me and I would pass it to my children. There was much to love about this land. Even small things like walking down the gravel roads, you could experience almost anything like roadrunners to horned toads to blue racers. The snakes would rise up, flare their heads like a cobra, and start chasing you down the fence line. I don't know who was frightened the most, you or the snake. I think the snake got the most excitement from the adventure.

Surprisingly enough, Della was with child again another girl we named her Lola Marie was born October 07, 1923. We decided to call her Marie and even though she was small in size, she made up for it by expressing big opinions. From early on, we could tell that Marie was a smart child and as she grew, we knew we could rely on her thoughts.

Soon after, Stella, being of age, became engaged to Elbert Lyday. Once engaged, she gave the impending marriage a lot of thought; she knew that a woman could honorably break off attachments for several reasons: incompatibility, ungentlemanly habits, inconsistency or ill temper. However, after much contemplation, she decided that marrying Elbert was what she wanted and in 1926 they were wed and moved to their home in upper part of the county.

In this era, many sought prohibition, especially the Democratic Party and in 1928, debates over legalization continued. The purchase of 3.2 percent beer legalized later and hard liquor could still be obtained through bootleggers. Della did not like all this propaganda and kept me upset over the issues. She was always reading something and wanting me to do something about them. Della and Stella's new husband would have debates over these issues and more. My wife was too thoughtful for women in these times, but I think her love of reading was what spurred her intelligence.

The wheat fields shimmered like golden silk in the sun. Tobacco grew in the next clearing, its long broad leaves tipped to catch the sunlight. Farther on, the yellow tassels of cornstalks wagged in the south breeze. Rising up from a squat at the end of the corn row, I felt pressure in my head directly on the spot where that darned mule kicked me years ago. Immediately, I put my hand on my head as I straightened up with the blood rushing to my head from the strain of the squat. The whole incident again brought to mind the day I was kicked and how this knot was still there. I didn't know why this pressure kept reoccurring, but no doctors here could explain it to me.

The hawks scoured over the fields in lazy spirals in search of prey. Riding closer, my son, Lloyd, halted his mare alongside my big gelding and we surveyed the fields together. He said, "The corn is getting taller. We should have a good crop." I was pleased that my sons cared for this land, too. Conscious of the sun's rays heating my back, I turned in the saddle, glanced at the sun shielding my eyes from its glare, and checked the location in the sky. With a sigh, I realized it was later than I thought. Reluctantly, I turned the gelding and we started for home.

Later that evening, Lloyd went to visit Edgar Woods; he asked him to stay for supper. He came home telling us a story about the chicken that was on his plate. He had a previous experience with a chicken that pecked him hard on his backside through the cracks while visiting their "out" house. He was hoping that maybe by some slim chance it was not the same one. We all laughed; Lloyd was always full of fun and loved to make folks happy.

Our next daughter to marry was Linnie. She married Archie Lyday, Elbert's brother, and moved to Atoka, Oklahoma in 1929. In that same year Della became saddened when her father passed away. He was a life long friend to Della in which she spent many unforgettable evenings talking and enjoying each others' company. Now, our children and I were all she had left. Even though I didn't know quite how to tell her, I felt for my wife and longed to make things better for her. Soon, though, things were a bustle again with Floyd marrying Lena Jackson. The wedding was a nice distraction for Della, but soon, the newlyweds moved to Bakersfield California, where Floyd started farming land there.

On the prairie, a drought started, which brought the dust that continued for many months and in the western part created dustbowls. The drought caused everyone a lot of losses. With no rains, the crops yielded less and it was hard to keep enough food for livestock and save enough for the family. The drought spread into 1931 and the ground was not ready for planting. We kept waiting for the rain that did not come until late in the year. The creek was a tepid trickle because of lack of rain. However, it was too late to plant a crop to harvest and when the winds begin to blow in the spring of 1932; it kept the grounds dry and unsuitable for planting.

The wind kept blowing and the dirt storms lasted day, after day, and the dirt began to build. In late January of 1933, the drought continued with blasts of wind and dirt to this arid climate. The temperature kept dropping and the wind and dirt was visible throughout the year. The dust and the storms lessened in 1934, but the heat created even more unpleasantness.

In 1935, Beulah married Burlin Richardson and moved to Bakersfield California; and in that same year, Lloyd married Thelma Smith. Another great storm came through and left black dirt everywhere. It was like the wind and dirt had been blowing forever, and this last huge cloud of dirt became known as Black Sunday. This experience taught us new farming methods and brought us to a new era in soil conservation. It taught the valuable lesson of how to take care of the land.

The depression was in full bloom and in 1936, our house burned to the ground. We lost everything, but a few animals that we were raising. Afterwards, I decided to borrow against the land and build across the road on the south side, which became the location of the new Newton Home.

This new home was the icon of the community and a memorable site of the Newton's on the Twelve-Mile Prairie. In the dining room, there was symmetry, simplicity, and a trove of stoneware that set the stage for friendly gatherings. Aged wooden surfaces and peeling paint complement the graceful ceramic forms displayed on the farmhouse hutch, along with the varied seating including mix and match side chairs.

I decided in that same year to dig a well and install a windmill that supplied water for the family needs and some livestock and water for the garden during dry seasons. The boys were all grown up and learning how to till the land and raise cattle so they found their own ways to expand new ideas.

One day, Della sat at the treadle machine and started cutting out remnants of the leftover of her cotton dress and made an apron with a bib on top for safeguarding her dress. When she hurried into the kitchen to prepare dinner, her apron was the first thing she reached for. It made a marvelous container for carrying in the eggs she gathered in the henhouse and sometimes for carrying fresh vegetables brought in from the garden. Della would lift the babies in to her apron and move them back and forth to keep them occupied. Other times, she would sit out on the porch with a mess of green beans to snap and use her apron as a basket. The apron had to be continuously washed and that wasn't simple either, as it required lugging in water from the well and scrubbing out stains on an old copper washboard, but it was better than down at the creek scrubbing the clothes on rocks that she had to do when she first arrived.

This prairie, where the deer and antelope played and where the buffalo roamed was the continuous remembrance of the presence of the Indians which occupied this territory, and what they gave for mankind to enjoy the peace of this homestead. Every year we enjoyed the Indian summers, seeing the clouds that were large and beautifully spaced made the evenings worthwhile. After the work was finished, this was a time for remembering the things that my father told me and the events of the family discussed and the plans for the New Year seemed the perfect time and opportunity.

Before long, our daughter Velia married Perry Studdard. She continued to help Della and me with work on the farm. Another year brought about sadness to everyone when father, George Washington Newton, passed away. We lay him to rest in the Rose Hill Confederate Cemetery in Ardmore Oklahoma, on October

5, 1939. Mourning the passing of an era, we composed his frame with an unerringly eye but his real gift was a piercing insight into the emotional story lines and their often cryptic and ironic subplots that teamed beneath the surface of our lives. In addition, the loss brought us back to the dreams mother and father set for us on this prairie.

Determined to carry the dream for generations, again, became my focus. My thoughts were to convey the need to ask my sons to stay and help work the land. I paused, letting the full weight of the question resonate while Della said my eye had a piercing gaze that gauged the reaction of my sons. Lloyd and Boyd accepted, knowing the great honor it would bring to be a part of this twelve-mile prairie. Pleased to have them to be apart of my accomplishments, I spoke and said, "Now, I own 320 acres of this prairie for farming and raising cattle. The body breaking toil, the tedium, the call to be tough was the battle for a living. This is my battlefield, and living in the country, that father fought with persistence and with pride made me proud to be American."

Presently, we introduced cotton along with all our other crops, like corn, wheat, and oats and started planting it every year. I hired more workers besides the family to work the farm. I now had eight teams working the fields and twenty-one head of milk cows and forty head of hogs. Della had one hundred laying hens and one hundred turkeys waiting for slaughter. The smokehouse was filled with hanging meat.

Della never left the kitchen until all the men were fed. Feeding the hire hands each day along with all the others, chores were shelling the corn with the corn Sheller. I took the corn and all the different grains we grew to town to be ground and brought back for Della in the kitchen. Every Friday, just like clockwork, I took the milk and the eggs to town and I never missed a Friday's trip to town. Bringing back blocked ice from the icehouse in Durant for the wooden icebox used to keep our food cold.

Lloyd was always experimenting and trying different crops. He talked me into planting tobacco in the spots where we burnt brush piles of trees that we cleared for farming in the bottomland by Bois d' Arc Creek. Velia was with child and delivered a baby girl on June 4, 1940, and they named her Shirley Ann she was born at home here on this farm. Working the cattle, Lloyd dismounted and started patting his horse on the neck. The animal was covered with lather and its sides were heaving as it gasped for air. Dick was with Lloyd and he stopped his horse and hooked one leg across the pommel of his saddle, and then sat there, looking down at Lloyd. Congratulating one another on a good job they had done moving the cattle, they pulled the herd up from the back pastures. We built working chutes and head gates in the corrals which made the work go faster it was easier to separate the bulls from the young heifers that we only let stay a couple of months for breeding.

Dick became our veterinarian, and that was what we called him since that job came to him by accident when he cared for some of our cattle that got sick one time. Therefore, he gave the livestock their shots, and castrated the livestock when needed.

Dick, married B.B. LaRue in January 31, 1947 and they moved one mile north of my land and started farming and raising cattle that he later purchased. Lloyd took over all the farming responsibilities of the land including the cattle. Marie married Doyle Allen and their first son Louie was born. Marie's second marriage was to Johnny Gardner, and this brought about another child a little girl, and they named her Brenda. She later divorced and remarried Doyle Allen and they had two more sons Lanny and Larry. Velia married Ernest "Bud" Allen in Durant in 1948 and moved to Borger, Texas. The next year we welcomed Patsy Dianna, a baby girl in May 22, 1949.

Lloyd continued to farm the land and grow the crops. Velia came back every year and helped Lloyd, Zora and Marie. Shirley and Patsy and Lloyd's children Janell, Dretha, Kay, Wayne, Jim and Elaine helped work the fields and keep the crops clean of grasses and collected the harvest every year.

Chapter 3

▼

Lloyd and Thelma

She was both Irish and Cherokee. As a girl, her dark brown hair swept sleekly back and she had the features that appeared sculpted by the hand of God. Her eyes were brown and her face as smooth as the finest ivory. She had satin skin and beautiful hands. I said, "I was told you have Cherokee blood, but you don't look like it." She answered and said, "They told me I was one-eighth Cherokee." A silence fell between us and we both turned our attention to the scenery. The setting was in the mist of the wide-open meadow, with the green thick carpet-like grass and bunches of wildflowers. Shifting my eyes toward her I said, "You are opposite of the Cherokee's. They have bronze skin and high cheekbones."

The saga continues with me, Lloyd Newton, courting Thelma Smith; born April 21, 1916, in Kenefic, Okla. Thelma was the most fascinating person that I had ever encountered. She always said all the right things and could dance, and knew all the latest steps and moves, liked music, and kept me captivated with her smile. It was destiny, I could feel it. She could do no wrong and I thought about her all the time. I also could not wait until the end of every week to go and be with her.

One evening, after leaving Thelma's house, it was late and I was riding Dad's horse. The road was dirt and I noticed a double row of trees. It was pitch-black and the road was visible for only a few feet in front of me. Suddenly, I heard a rustling sound from the trees, and above me something unexpectedly jumped out of the tree and slapped the back of the horse. The horse suddenly became frightened and almost threw me. I managed to hang on and when I looked around, I saw this black panther. I was petrified and the next thing I remember was getting off the horse in front of the house. Still alive, I thought I had better check my pants! Every one in the house was asleep and I didn't want to awake anyone. I was still keyed up so it was impossible to go to sleep, as I was thinking about the panther and how it might have followed me back to the house. My instincts were to get a gun and maybe I could shoot it, but that would just wake everyone in the house.

The next day I checked the horse, and it had scratches where the panther had clawed its back. From that point on when riding at night, especially in the covered tree area, I would get goose bumps and that same daunting feeling that never goes away. However, I didn't let that keep me from seeing my Thelma until dark. A few months passed and Thelma became intrigued by the Brush Arbors in our area and started attending the services. Clyde Petty, a prestigious evangelist, came and started preaching. In one of the meetings Thelma received the Holy Spirit, and gave her life to Christ.

Our lives began to change. This excitement made everything seem better. I wanted to be with Thelma all the time and I knew that we were getting closer. "Time will tell," I said, "But, I am going to have you! You are going to be my wife." I kept repeating the words softly, reverently to my future wife. Finally, on December 28, 1935, we were married in Durant, Oklahoma. We took up residence at the old house on Dad's place that was located on the north side of the road not far from Mrs. McGinnis that was up on the hill a little piece from us. Father's home was just beyond the ridge, a short distance. The responsibility of working the land became mostly mine, although Dad insisted he perform his share of the work.

The prelude of summer began and in the area beside the house where we lived, there was no water except for down at Bois d' Arc Creek. This creek was just a short distance from the house. Thelma used it to wash the clothes and carry water for cleaning. The honing sun couldn't be any sweeter on the billowing sheets on the clothesline. The sunlight and the good smell of fresh-cut grass from the newly mowed lawn made me thirsty for a drink of water from Dad's well that I brought over to our place in the evenings.

In this area of the country, the neighbors were far apart and the summer nights were hot just like tonight. I was sitting out on the porch with Thelma. It was a quiet night and we were looking at God's lantern that was shinning bright; we noticed there was something in the road headed our way in the distance. I said, "Thelma do you see something coming?" Thelma suddenly stood up and said, "Shoosh, be quiet Lloyd. It looks like two men walking this way." We immediately ran into the house and hid behind the door, both of us looking around the door as if to see what was going to happen next. You never knew when undesirable folks might be coming to do no harm. All of the sudden, Thelma shouted, "Oh Lloyd, it's a Cow!" We laughed at ourselves for being so silly.

We were limited of some degree for things to do at night. The rooms were illuminated by the glow of coal oil lamps. I played the harmonica and guitar, while Thelma would read her Bible until time to retire for bed. Into our second year of marriage, Thelma was showing signs of being in the family way and delivered a baby girl on January 2, 1937. We were so excited and overwhelmed by having a child of our own. She was a beautiful blonde-headed green-eyed miracle in her own right. She was delivered by Dr. Jennings at our home. This was our first addition to the family and we named her Janell. She was the second grandchild for William and Della born on this property and we were delighted with her presence.

Life at home became more important with every new day! Janell became everything to us. Having a family was what I had always wanted and Thelma liked to brush her hair, dress her up and make a big doing over her, and this pleased me a lot.

The winters were very cold and living in this old house made me long for the feeling of spring. Thelma heated bricks and placed them at the foot of the bed to keep our feet warm through the long winter nights. A sudden gust of wind would rattle the windows and the days seemed drawn out and endless, especially when it snowed and there wasn't much to do except feed the livestock and break the frozen pond for the livestock to have a drink of water.

The smell of wood smoke perfumed the air that was coming out of the chimney from the top of the house. I used the axe often to cut wood for the stove which was easier when I found dead trees to chop down that were already dried and cured. Times were unyielding for us and no one around us had little to speak of but we managed to survive the winter.

In the spring of the New Year, while visiting a friend who had some young pups, we chose a lively new pet and brought him home for Janell. We named him Ralph and he was black and white with long hair; he looked like a mixed-breed collie. Ralph was a good-natured dog, and Janell took up with him; but, he always liked to tag along with me.

It was in the early part on 1938, when we moved to a little place called Brown, just a few miles from the home place. Walter Smith, Thelma's brother, came and lived with us. I had a small piece of land and let Walter use my horse to cultivate it. There was no work after the depression; therefore, President Roosevelt started up the WPA and I got a job and started to work. This helped by putting food on the table and enough money to buy a few things we needed. We moved back to Dads place in 1939. Walter built a barn for my cow, which meant a lot to Thelma, and me. After a few months, Walter started a career in the military. Next, we moved to Mr. Linville's old place just down from Tick Creek between Mrs. McGinnis and Jim and Bee Perkins in 1940.

Thelma was expecting and this time we were hopeful for a boy, but on March 2, 1940, Mrs. Slack, the mid wife, delivered another beautiful girl. We named her Dretha, and she was dark headed and had beautiful brown eyes. The first thing people said at their first glimpse of Dretha was, "Lloyd, we know this one is yours ... she has those Newton eyes." Janell was now three years old and just big enough that Thelma still had to keep a constant eye on both her and the baby. Our family was beginning to grow. Living was more complicated with each new day tilling the same soil that had been in the family for years. Suddenly, one day I looked up from my work and became startled by the beauty of the place. A gentle breeze carried the sweet sounds of nature over the fields. This combination of country farmland and woodland gave me an ongoing feel of affection for the outdoors. The years seemed to pass more rapidly and the days appeared to shorten with all this family activity.

Thelma was with child once more and started labor on April 20, 1944 and I drove her to the Haney hospital in Durant where Dr. Haney delivered a girl we named Linda Kaye. Linda was another beautiful girl, and she too, had those Newton brown eyes. Janell and Dretha became little moms to Kaye, and insisted that they take care of her. Having her around gave them another plaything and they were always making over her as if she was a baby doll. Another girl meant a lot to all of us, and brought us closer as a family, and there was never a dull moment.

It became additional work for Thelma caring for the girls and later in the year, she became ill. Soon, she began having problems breathing and had taken pneumonia. Complication from the pneumonia developed into a more serious situation called tuberculosis. With the help from family and friends, I was able to take Thelma to a hospital in Talihina for treatment. Thelma kept coughing, and spitting up parts of her lungs, until in the process she lost a half of her lung, and stayed in the hospital for nine months.

During this period in time, our close friends Lucille and Harold Mc Donald came over and asked to keep Kaye. Wonderful as it seemed that Lucille and

Harold wanted to do this for us, we were sad to have our child live with others. However, I was grateful and could use the encouragement and this typified the good-hearted nature of country people. Our little Kaye cried for days upon leaving us, and Lucille was just about to give up when Kaye finally adjusted to them, and things became easier for a while.

While Thelma was at the hospital, Janell and Dretha stayed with William and Della, during the day, and the nights with me. The nights were sleepless ones, and I was constantly thinking about Thelma and the children. I began to feel that nothing was right anymore. This led me to consider what would Thelma want me to do. Remembering her words took me to my knees, I begin to pray, and ask God for help, and day after day it seemed that there was no way out of these circumstances.

Knowing I could not just give up, this prairie suddenly became more important to me and it consumed my thoughts. I ached for a little normality and my mundane work on the land helped provide that for me. Finally, the word came that Thelma was strong enough to come home, and I could not wait to be with her, and just hold her, in my arms. When she walked in the door of our home, she looked around and started to cry. I took her hand and said, "What's wrong, you're crying." She said, "I was thinking that I would never see our home and my family again." This brought tears to my eyes and I turned and faced her, reaching down to take her hand in an attempt to offer what comfort I could. She turned into the shelter of my arms. Holding her, I knew there was no other place I wanted to be but right here on this farm with my loving wife and family.

At this point, it was obvious that while I thought we were suffering here at home, it was really Thelma who had endured the most. She had always seemed to be weak in her body and now, she was even frailer. Everyone knew about Thelma's upbringing and how it was a hard one. She always worked hard since losing her mother and father early in life and many times went to bed hungry. She also told me that J.C., someone in her family, had jumped into her back when she was a young girl and this had caused many of her problems.

These thoughts lingered and after a while I walked off into the woods trying to clear my head, but what kept reoccurring to me was the trauma that Thelma had been through and I knew that she would never be the same. Now, I felt helpless, day after day, her body never seemed to improve. Most of the time, she felt weak and could not stand for any length of time on her feet without having to sit or lay down. The least bit of exertion would tear the lining of her lung, and it would start bleeding again. Frustration set in. "This was it!" I could not dismiss her uncertainties and now I knew wild horses couldn't drag me away from her and I was determined to protect her at all cost.

The situation intensified my expectation it was as if we needed the struggles to stretch our capability and sorrows to appreciate the laughter and the boredom to discover joy in small blessings. Every worthwhile accomplishment, big or little had its stages of drudgery and triumph, a beginning, a struggle, and a victory. Now, Thelma became dependent on all the family, and we used her wisdom to educate us. She learned the limits of her body, and knew just what to do to survive. It was at this pinnacle in her life, she became a regular to the church.

Thelma began to try by all means necessary, to gain her strength. Some one told her that if she would drink raw eggs with milk, that it would help her to gain weight. To get stronger she took their advice, it worked, her breathing was better, and she had more energy and slowly increased her workload. Just when Thelma commenced to get stronger, Lucille and Harold brought Kaye home after she had stayed with them for three years. Bringing Kaye home was difficult for Lucille and Harold; it was if she become their own child. There was not a dry eye in the house. It was very touching seeing a grown man cry. The feelings were overwhelming for the family and just to have our family all together was more than words could express.

Thelma had many friends in the community starting with her very closest, including Juanita Woods, Lucille McDonald, Velma McDonald, Mary Reynolds, Bee Perkins, and Mrs. Slack, all which went to her church and became very supportive. Thelma never wanted to miss church; in order for her to go, she would have to get a ride with Mr. and Mrs. Slack who owned a Model T Ford.

Not all the children would get to go because of the limited seating. As a result, they took turns and this was a treat for them because it was twelve miles to Durant where they went to church. Sometimes the children would obtain a ride with Jim and Bee Perkins. Jim drove a pickup truck, and the kids had to ride in the back. The wind would blow their hair, which became a problem because they did not want a hair out of place. However, if you wanted to go, this was the way it was going to be.

Sometimes I sent the girls, walking from our house to Jim and Bee's house who lived on the same dirt road we did. The problem was they lived about two miles down the road and going south on one side of the road was Mr. Linville's land and the other side was Mr. Self's place. Both of them had large bulls who wanted to fight. The bulls would stomp the ground, and kick up dirt in the air. The girls were deathly afraid of these large animals, and the bulls knew it. When the girls came down the road, the bulls came closer and closer to the fence. The girls were so terrified that they crawled on hands and knees in the ditch until they passed them. The girls didn't care too much for the old house either, especially when they discovered that there were other inhabitants besides the family, and they were terrified to see them moving behind the wallpaper. Janell shouted, "Look Daddy, it's a rat!" I would have to call in the dogs and they would chase the rat until they killed it.

Time passed quickly and Thelma was with child again. This time, I had myself resigned to the fact that it would be another girl, but instead, out came a boy. This was one of the happiest days of my life. I finally got a son, on August 4, 1948, born at the Evergreen Hospital in Durant. We named him Loyd Wayne, he was blonde headed, and of course, had those Newton eyes. We called him "cotton top" and the girls took turns spoiling him and used him as a way of getting out of their chores. Janell took responsibility of keeping Wayne, and he slept with her. In the thick of all this madness, Thelma was pregnant again and delivered another son on August 13, 1949. We named him Boyd Dayne; he was born with a birth defect, his fingers were grown together just like Stella's and mine. I did not hesitate to say how wonderful I felt. The reality of how great it was having another son. I had waited so long for boys and now I had two, so close to each other.

In the same month that Dayne was born, Wayne was in the first stages of walking and we noticed he did not want to use his left leg, and would try to drag it. We took him to a general practitioner and he was diagnosed with Polio. We were instructed to take him to the Catholic hospital in Tulsa, Oklahoma for treatment.

The cure for Polio was still in the experimental stages. We were told that Polio started by contracting a virus. Blood samples had to be taken from Wayne to test his condition. The hospital staff explained to us that Franklin Roosevelt was one of the best-known Polio victims. He was the one responsible and gave the approval for Dr. Jonas Salk to develop a polio vaccine for the National Foundation for Infantile Paralysis. Salk developed a vaccine that had been tested and started giving it to humans mostly boys and girls that had contracted the disease. The staff started the treatments on Wayne; he went through a series of injections. Later we were told that over 58, 000 Americans had contracted the disease. We were in desperate hopes they would conquer this dreaded thing that was in epidemic proportions. Eventually, though, the cure came and my family was indebted to God, Franklin Roosevelt and Dr Jonas Salk and anyone else responsible for saving my little boys life.

Wayne received a crippled children's card and continued therapy. Thelma was distressed that Wayne was still in the hospital and away from everyone he knew. This kept her heart broken. Just the thought that no one was there with him just intensified the situation. There were long periods of time that we were unable to see him and sometimes that it was a month or more. Wayne would perk up and stand up in his crib when we walked into his room. However, the moment we told him goodbye, his little legs would collapse and he would fall, crying, and the sound echoed thru out the hospital. Thelma would cry all the way home, too, and I sometimes wondered how much more our family could endure. Unfortunately, I was about to find out.

During the time Wayne was receiving treatment, Dayne got pneumonia and when we took him to the doctor he was also diagnosed with polio. We were all panic-stricken that such a thing could happen to our family. We took him to the same hospital in Tulsa where Wayne was being treated. Dayne got worse and then the unbearable happened; he passed away. Thelma rested her cheek against the wool of my coat, letting it absorb her tears. Thelma's lips quivered, as she whispered, "Little Dayne died." More tears came after a deep breath. I drew back and self-consciously wiped the tears from my cheeks. This was our Easter Sunday in 1950, the saddest day of my life when my baby boy was no longer with me. He was just eight months old and my heart was heavy with grief. The children resented his passing and expressed their feelings to their mother.

Later in the year, Thelma, who had found out she was pregnant shortly after Dayne's passing, started labor pains and I took her to the hospital were she delivered another baby boy. He was born on December 08, 1950 and we named him Jimmy Harold. The ambience of the home shifted to joy and the children showered him with attention. Jimmy being born made me a very happy man. He kept the family delighted with his presence. Wayne was home now, too, and having these two boys brought some joy into our lives again.

Into the next year, Lucille McDonald became pregnant, delivered a son to their family, and named him Kenny. This was an awesome thing for all of us since we were all like family and Lucille would bring him over for visits. Time seemed to be on our side and life became somewhat normal. Jimmy liked to visit my Dad, and he, too, was smitten with Jimmy and nicknamed him "Jimbo". The name took hold and soon everyone called him by that name. Jimmy adopted the name and always liked to go visit Grandpa Newton, the name all the kids called him at that time.

Wayne was very curious of all things and had this habit of cocking his eyebrow to one side and that got the attention of a friend of ours from church, Mr. Mayo.

He was always giving him things and spoiling him. We would put Wayne to bed with his bag of marbles. He insisted on sleeping with them and one time, in the middle of the night, he lost one of his marbles and began to cry. This went on and on until we finally found his marble. Needless to say, there was no sleeping if Wayne lost his marbles. We joked about that for years.

Subsequently, Thelma was pregnant again and delivered a baby girl on December 02, 1953. We named her Sharon Elaine and everyone had to spoil her. Elaine was the most beautiful baby you had ever seen and she brought joy to all of us. Now, Elaine being the youngest received all the attention of everyone. All of us let her get by with things that the rest of the children didn't get to, like sucking her thumb, which went on for years until Reverend South promised if she would stop he would buy her a complete toy dish set. To our amazement, this bribe worked.

The girls were getting older and the house was bustling with activity. We were going more places, more often and just before going to town, Thelma would tell the girls to go and put on their newest undergarments. She was fearful they would have an accident, and in the process be taken to the hospital with old garments; she had such pride in those days. I remember, too, another funny tale of my wife. She would tell the girls to go and wash their "pie pans", an expression meaning their most private parts. To the girls, this was the most embarrassing figure of speech; it turned their complexion slightly pink. Poor Thelma couldn't bring it on her self to repeat the parts of the female anatomy. From then on, the word "pie pan" was taboo in our family and whenever Thelma used the word, the girls would get embarrassed. However, the men in the family received the most amusement.

As odd is it may seem, life was never boring out in a place like this, in fact, the remoteness lent to the drama many times. One evening, it was immediately before dark and the girls were outside playing. I heard a scream that pierced the night and then another that sounded like a wolf, howling. Another scream later and Dretha burst through the door yelling, "It's a wolf and I think it's got Linda." I ran out the door, there was Linda, on her hands and knees with her mouth wide open, and no sound coming out. She was in shock and trying to get up on the porch but going nowhere. So I looked around, trying to find out what is was and reduce the urgency a little. To my surprise, the only "wolf" I could find was Boyd's old coonhound, obviously as scared to death of Linda as she was of him. Boyd's ole' coonhound ran across the field and to this day no one has seen him since. Funny things a person can see in the dark.

As the kids grew, our experiences with them changed. Later the same year the girls saw a "wolf" at our place, Thelma and I went into town for supplies and upon arriving home, Linda met us at the car and told us what happened while we were away. She explained that just after we left, Dretha began to ask the others if we were gone yet. She said, "I knew Dretha was up to something." So, she went into the dining room and Dretha was standing at the mirror and cutting her hair. Linda explained, "She did it swiftly and ruthlessly before the mirror, not meeting her own eyes, grasping each long strand, now lying on the worn linoleum floor." Then, she told us Dretha lifted her head to the mirror. Her hair hung in tatters around her face, stopping a few inches below her ears. Dretha told Linda that in her mind, she saw soft, tumbling waves drifting around her head. They would make her eyes larger, she had explained to Linda. Then Linda said, "I took a deep breath to push down the nausea, and said aloud to Dretha. What in the world have you done to your hair?" Then Dretha said, after taking another breath, "Obviously, Linda, I have cut my hair!" Maybe you've heard of a haircut?" Then Linda said, with a worried look on her face, "I heard of hair cuts. That is not a haircut. That looks like you put a bowl over your head and started whacking. Mom's going to have a heart attack and I don't want to be you when Daddy finds out." Linda went on to tell us, speaking ever so rapidly, "I asked Dretha, what are you going to do about church?" Dretha had just said, "I'm not going to church. I'm tired of that, too." This was about the time we had arrived.

At the end of Linda's frantic tattling, Dretha came out for the big unveiling. By this time, Thelma was sitting with her mouth wide open, she began turning her head from side to side as she looked at Dretha. Dretha shot Thelma a dark look and I walked over closer to Dretha, it was obvious she would rather die than cry. I couldn't help but feel Thelma's disappointment. Dretha, knowing she was in trouble, said, "Daddy, it was a mistake. I don't know why I did it." When I didn't say anything, she smiled and looked at Linda and said, "Well, if I get a whipping it won't hurt but a little while and I'll still have my short hair." She looked at me again and said, "All the girls are cutting their hair now." Her mother spoke up and said, "That doesn't mean you have the right to do what you please." Then I told her to go to her room until her mother and I had time to discuss what to do about her. Dretha got her short hair but suffered the consequences.

Several weeks had passed since Dretha's rebellion and Linda must have been gotten a little jealous over her sister's new look. I finally discovered what the girls had been up to. Dretha boldly confessed to me that she had convinced Linda to cut her hair too. She had said, "Linda, let me cut you some bangs and they will never know if you pull them to one side while in their presence." Dretha had gone on to explain to her sister how good they would both look with cut hair and a good tan. Linda told me, "She had me convinced from the word go." The girls knew that their mother would not permit any kind of sun bathing, so Dretha thought up this great idea to put on some shorts first and put regular clothes over them. Over the arc of the emerging sun to the fields, they went and as soon as they arrived at the field, they had pulled everything off down to the shorts.

Needless to say, my daughters weren't as brilliant as they thought, because this attempt at sunbathing had left them scorched. They desperately tried to hide the burn from their mother and me, but they later confessed that their night was miserable and they had tried everything from their's mother's cold cream to anything else they could find. I got the girls up early the next morning and sent them back to the fields. Everything that touched the burn just intensified the hurt and they were walking slow trying not to rub the burn. The girls were unaware that they looked like a couple of ducks waddling. The girls were always getting into some kind of trouble for one thing to another, especially Dretha.

One morning, I woke early to find a spider's web under construction on the front porch and dreamily looked out on the light mist in the air. Stubby, our half terrier, rubbed up against me trying to be friendly, his bright eyes flashing knowing that breakfast was just about to happen. Heading to the barn, I took in a breath of the fresh morning air. I loved days like this. I heard footsteps on the gravel behind me and I looked back to see Wayne, following me, as I wondered why would he be up and out of bed already. The thought came about the same time Wayne spoke. He said, "You promised to take us fishing today if it rained." My Irish skin flushed slightly, I chuckled with relief and we headed to the river.

In mid stream leaping fish glinted silver in the sun. While baiting hooks, I watched my son's excitement. Fishing was one way to liven Wayne up. I knew he thought of this river every year at this time. Wayne had the soul of his father, that was for sure! It was his birthday today and he was excited that we had found some time away together.

The sweltering August heat lingered, making sleep impossible. While we were away, Thelma had gone off on a walk by herself. That evening, she relayed to me the details of her day. She said that she had lain in the cool grass. While everyone was away, she felt a whistling breeze floating across the spacious meadow. She said that she had walked into a field of Indian paintbrushes, the wind enabling the wildflowers and grass to dance to the symphony of sounds. She had passed the creek, reminding her of the hot summer afternoons when she had played there with the children, wading in the cool water and catching fireflies just down from the creek by the old oak tree where there was always a field of butter cups and bees hovering over some open flower petals.

She told me of how she felt in love with the lands potential and admired its friendly southern breezes. She had observed clusters of blackbirds foraging for seeds around a heard of cattle grazing and a faint crow call in the distant. It was as if she were in a trance, the minutes turned into hours. I knew that all the times laid up in that hospital it took a Herculean effort to recall all of this, to recover that intensity but it is precisely the prodigious effort required to remind her of all of this. Now, with her telling me all of her experiences today in such detail, I knew that she was soaking up every experience like this she was allowed. My wife must have never known how many days like this she had left.

It wouldn't be long now until Winter was upon us. We have so many fond memories of times near that season. The family remembers and we never let her forget when Dretha had her experience with the last bottle of ketchup. There was only one trip to the grocery once a week and some times longer and Dretha was saving this bottle for hard times. Dretha had a craving for this stuff she loved. While the children were passing it around the table, Dretha turns and grabbed the bottle, in her passion of the excitement she dropped the last bottle of ketchup. It splattered all over the kitchen floor. She became upset and ran to her room crying.

Winter also meant it was close to Christmas and the children were overwhelmed of the essence of Christmas as Thelma and I always made it special for them. If we were lucky, the feathery snow would lie a foot deep, fresh-fallen, on the still countryside and in the woods just below our home. Indoors, the fire is glowing on the hearth and the grown ups and the children patiently awaiting the evening of the night before Christmas. To the south was a white woods forever silent. It was thought there were no humans at all in any direction but our own family. Christmas Eve drew a magic circle around the members of our family.

Lucille and Harold McDonald brought Kenny over to open gifts, this was a delight for Kenny to watch us open our gifts. Before opening gifts, we expressed what Christmas meant to us. Then we prayed as a family, along with the stories, laughter and food.

December's winter solstice signals the longest night of the year instinctively, we yearn for warmth and illumination, for the radiant glow of flickering candlelight. Christmas Day presented itself with the persuasive melody of my voice humming a carol. Our house was made for music, listening to the songs echo holding Christmas dear to our hearts. The delusions of our childish day, we recall it is the rule a carol that evokes the spirit of Christmas.

I had previously purchased a large basket of fruit the smell of fresh apples, oranges, lemons, limes, bananas, pineapples, and coconut. The coconut had a special meaning to all of us. The children couldn't wait until I punched the eyes of the coconut and drained the juice and give each one of them their portion and then I cracked open the coconut and shared each piece with the children.

We also indulged in the pears that Ruby, Thelma's sister, sent over from her pear trees. She individually wrapped each one and they were always delicious. Lastly, we purchased a second basket full of all kinds of nuts. This was the only time of the year we were fortunate to receive this kind of reward.

Christmas was the time of year to go pick the mistletoe and place it mystically over the door for all the guest and friends to enjoy its ambiance. Thelma had starched and ironed her lace collar given to her by her mother. She had taken special care with her hair that morning because this was Christmas.

"What smells so good? Does it not smell delicious?" The aroma coming from the kitchen was a brown sugar pineapple ham, hen, and dressing with all the trimmings. Looking over at the dessert table, I noticed pecan pies, chocolate pies and banana pudding. My eyes burned into Thelma's from across the room. Suddenly there was no longer that elusive sense of something missing. There was excitement in the house and happiness. Christmas was somehow complete.

Later the girls asked if they could stay up. "Not even one more minute," I told them. The girls were giggling and trying to lie at the foot of the bed. Thelma told everyone goodnight. I grinned down at her and said that goodnight sounded good to me. I nestled into the bed and thought, Thelma and only Thelma forever. "Mm," she said and snuggled against me. I said, "This feather bed doesn't compare in comfort to how I feel right now." I kissed her, with my lips lingering on hers, she said, "Merry Christmas, Lloyd." She closed her eyes and I sighed with warm contentment.

Chapter 4

▼

My Experience

Born, Latitude: 335938N and Longitude:0962214W, my ship sailed north twelve-miles and set anchor in the prairie my father as captain and my mother co-captain, the community rich in land used for farming and cattle ranches. Over 100 years has transpired since the birth of my Great Grandfather Newton, the fourth generation continues with me, Loyd Wayne Newton, born on this prairie and accepting responsibilities that my father Lloyd, and grandfather William labored diligently to preserve the heritage set before them. At an early age, I was introduced to the agricultural phenomenon. I was taught the basics with access to the wide-open skies and the rivers, lakes, and forest big enough you could get lost.

From the beginning, I studied under the greatest people that ever lived, my parents. The wisdom they instilled at adolescence positioned my adulthood and helped me discover my identity. Mother always encouraged me to be myself and said that God loves everyone the same and that he was no "respecter of person." She also said we were all the same in his eyes. She taught me that love leaves a legacy and knowing your purpose motivates your life. She said life without God makes no sense and we were put here to prepare for eternity.

Mother prayed every morning before we left home and asked Jesus to watch over us, keep us safe and bring us back home to her everyday. Mornings were not the only time my mother prayed, sometimes during the day, I would walk in our home and overhear her thanking God for everything in her life and for all the people around her. Still today, living on her prayers … what a legacy she has left for me, that is something that you cannot replace or put a dollar amount on. The wonderful part is she created a significant focus that radically altered the value God set for my existence. Mother stood in for me, replicating love that will last forever. She said, "Son, your home is a sanctuary, a place to retreat for privacy from the outside world … a place for prayer and regeneration." I always felt the Holy Spirit when she was around me! She revealed Gods love in her everyday experience in her walk with Him. I never underestimated the power of her spoken word.

My father, the gentle unassuming man with the elfin grin and twinkle in his eyes, plied his passion for the land, a verdant sanctuary of his creations. Dad, a common person with uncommon talent, born a natural with plants, said that vegetation is the fabric that brings color, comfort and reconnects us to nature. The meadows were a wildlife sanctuary and the orchards were filled with fruit trees, symbolizing the property's abundance through the ages and the links to the land to people gone by. Father would sometimes pause to inspect the subtle hue of one flower or stoop to inhale the sweet fragrance of another. I am sure he saw their beauty as a stunning testimony to nature and as evidence of God's best work. I, too, had gained his appreciation for plant life.

Mother and Father both had a special altruistic manner that they possessed and passed it down to all the children. A trait that we inherited became a good quality in all of their children. The mornings at home started with the same mundane expression, "The roosters were announcing the start of the day!" Dad, an early riser, would say, "I'm going to the barn to milk the cow, and I would like some breakfast when I get back." Mother always said, "Okay, but don't let anything get in that milk before you get back."

One morning, as Dad walked out of the house on the way to the barn, he noticed the ole' milk cow was in the pasture with the bitter weeds, sour dock, milkweeds pods and the Jimson weeds. He said that he just knew that one of us boys must have left the gate unlocked again. Dad started back to the house and I knew I was in trouble when he opened the door, "Son, did you leave that gate open last night?" I said, "I don't think so, why? Then he said someone left it open and Miss Bee is in there eating those bitter weeds. I looked over at Dad and said, "I'm sorry, Dad." He said, "Well, don't let it happen again." I said okay. Dad looked over at mother and said, "The milk is going to be bitter and I'll have to give it to the pigs." Luckily, we had some fresh milk left from the evenings milking last night. The smell of country bacon was in the air, I sat down at the table, there were wide strips of bacon and white gravy with homemade biscuits and hen eggs cooked over easy, and of course, cow's milk at our breakfast table.

At our place, you could hear the predawn choruses of wolves. Near daybreak, in spring, it was the waking songs and calls of quail, doves, red-birds, mockingbirds, chickadees, woodpeckers, and wrens. Later in the day, closer to dusk, the bullbats, bats, and chimmeysweeps came out from hiding and swarmed overhead. Out in the country, you were never far from nature and its' sounds.

One of the things I remember most about Daddy was his hands. They were rough and strong, they sustained a family with work and play. His hands were weathered from years of milking cows, making hay, chopping wood, picking corn, pulling on horses' reins and all his duties of this farm. Dad's handshake was as good as his word. His word stood for honor and integrity. He never met a soul that he didn't already know.

Nameless items, he called "whicker bills." He would say, "It just needs a new whicker bill." Witticisms seemed to roll off his tongue as naturally as a song pours out of a meadowlark's throat. This was a good interim time of life remembering Father's witticisms and my juvenile activities.

My own memories are varied and comical most times. I remember one Sunday after church, one of Mothers friends asked her over for Sunday lunch and I was able to come along. After lunch, Mother asked if I wanted to take a nap, which I really didn't want to do, but to please my mother, I said okay. She prepared a place on the floor for me. While on the floor, I found a cameo locket laying there and started playing with it. Somehow, it ended up in my mouth and I swallowed it. Immediately, I thought, "I'm going to die." I was so scared. I did not say anything to Mother because I was afraid she would spank me and that would be embarrassing.

Several hours passed and nothing happened. We went to church that night and I sat closely by mother's side, as I just knew I would die any minute. After church, we went home. Mother put me to bed; I just knew it would be the death of me before morning. The next morning, I awoke, and to my surprise, my heart was still beating. I could breath, but my next thought was what will happen to the inside of me? I wondered if the cameo would be inside me forever or ruin my insides. Then, fear came over me again as it occurred to me that the cameo might pass through me. Later in the day, to my astonishment, the cameo came out. I knew right then that I was going to be all right. Mother never knew the trauma that I experienced and I was to embarrassed to tell her!

One of my first responsibilities was gathering eggs in the hen house. Walking inside, the air was heavy, thicker than it had been outside. It smelled of straw and chicken feathers. I gathered an egg by reaching my hand underneath the softness of a hen sitting contentedly in a nest. With a suspicious "brraack?" the hen readjusted her position on the straw. The next hen was different; she had an abrupt-tone of the hen clucking. She pulled up with a wild "Aaaawk!" and her pointed beak of steel drilled my arm as she dove for my throat.

In the excitement, I crushed the egg in my fist and its contents ran down my upraised forearm in a slimy yellow stream. With shrieks, squawks, and a riot of fluttering wings, the chicken house became chaos. Clumsy hens flew in all directions thudding into the walls and knocking each other senseless in swirling storms of feathers. Spitting feathers, I covered my head with both arms and came out as quickly as possible. The weathered door banged open, bouncing off the wall of the old chicken house and I looked around hoping no one was looking at my first attempt to gather eggs.

The thickly leaved branches of the towering oak trees blocked the rays of the sun and cased a small premature darkness of the backside of the schoolhouse. The school hours were firmly established. The first class started at eight o'clock in the morning. One thing I will always remember about school was stating the pledge of allegiance, how patriotic we were, and how it made me feel. I was ready to start going to school and was excited every year thereafter.

Before starting, I was required to have all my inoculations. The thought of having to take more shots was a quick reminder of all those I had in the past. I had my share of the polio vaccine at the Catholic hospital in Tulsa. I was cured of polio, but the school nurse insisted that she listen with her stethoscope and I have the shots. Before it was over, she gave me the sugar cubes, as well.

I started Cobb Elementary in 1954. My first and second grade teacher was Mrs. Rambo. The third and fourth grade teacher was Mrs. Sims. I liked school and my teachers and especially recess and the laugher of the children. Our community was so small that we children were grouped together with a couple of grades in one classroom. We still had only about 20 children per class on average.

Some of the benefits of going to school was going over to Grandmother Newton's house in the afternoon. She met me at the door and said, "Son, are you hungry?" Of course, I was hungry and this was Grandmother's place, so I said yes and she set me down at the table. She promptly placed a plate before me with juicy fried chicken, golden corn bread and pan fried taters. Now if you have never had a piece of her bread, you don't know that it is the best ever. Not even Grandpa knew the family secret recipe. It is said that Grandma told him once, but he wasn't listening. She said, "How is your Mother?" I said, "She's good, Grandmother." Turning to one side, I saw Aunt Zora coming in from the barn.

Zora was an unflinching observer of like whose ability to penetrate the heart and soul of a wild array of characters revealed a fearless imagination. She liked her snuff and would contently take a pinch between cheek and gum. Grandmother asked me, "Would you like some more?" I said, "No thank you! That was very good; however, I would like some of that Kool-Aid." She gave me a glass filled about half the way and said, "I have some cookies if you would like one. I said yes, ate the cookie, and left saying thanks.

In the same era, Mrs. McGinnis, our close neighbor, lived up on the hill from us. She sent word for Lloyd's children to come to her house for something special she wanted to give us. When we arrived there, we noticed all shapes and sizes of gourds. There were gourds made into dippers use for dipping water or liquid. There were gourds made into birdhouses and some hanging from strings. She had invited because she had some cantaloupes to give us. After we visited for a while, we told her bye and started home with all the cantaloupes. The cantaloupes were very ripe and you could smell that aroma for what seemed like a quarter mile away.

While walking down the graveled road, suddenly, a large swarm of bumblebees came by us. We started running and our little hearts were pounding so fast I thought we were going to have a cardiovascular attack. We were almost home when, to our surprise, the bees came swarming again but this time they lit all over the ripe cantaloupes. I was terrified and started slapping, screaming, and jumping. My thoughts were to run and that is exactly what we all did. I became psyched for life, to this day, the smell of a cantaloupe almost turns my stomach, and I still refuse to eat cantaloupe.

There were various duties on the farm and one was shucking corn. We feed all the livestock grains from the farm. Inside the barn were bins for storing grains and corn was one of them. While going through the shucking process, you could see the slant of a sunbeam laden with thousands of dust particles that were visible through the cracks of the old barn. It was easy to see all the dust we were breathing and not really think about it when the sun wasn't there.

There were a myriad of ways to get in touch with wildlife on the prairie, especially the fastest raptors on this prairie, the hawks and owls. Or hear something making awful sounds and generally it would be a raucous mockingbird harassing a blue jay that was chasing a squirrel up the Bois d' Arc tree were it was storing a pecan found under the pecan trees. In addition, at the same time, a scissortail would fly by and they began to fight leaving the winner ludicrously overdone! A tinge of territorial imperative at work.

It was 9:00 a.m., January 10, 1958, in class at school when my sister came for me. I knew something was wrong and no one would tell me until I got home. When we got there, Dad told me Della, my Grandmother Newton had passed away. She went to the smokehouse to pick up a ham for everyone's lunch and had a heart attack on the way back. This was the first time that someone close to me had died and my heart was broken. I knew I would never see her again and started to cry and felt isolated.

Grandmother's passing brought to mind the huge picture in the large frame that always hung in the living room. Mr. Mayo gave it to us and it was called "Peace In The Valley." My thoughts were, will there ever be a place like that ... is that heaven? Maybe I will see Grandmother there some day!

The spirits of the Indians were always present and never absent from this prairie and as young boys, this gave us time to think of their way of life and the stance left behind of such great people that inhabited this land. Appropriately enough, this opened our imaginations to the unmentioned magic that was in the air. I know there is no one alive as crazy as we were as boys.

For us, swimming was always the "thing" to do. It was a great source of freedom and excitement for us. The native feelings ascended in us like free spirits of this prairie. Old Father Time visited us, which was a willing participant in the hopes that this experience would never end. What completes the reverie is the thought of that secluded getaway nestled in the trees, our favorite swim hole.

One February, we had a mischievous flash, just a minute layer of ice was present on the creek. We just had to go swimming! About a half mile away from the house, on Bois d' arc Creek, our favorite swimming hole, the water was twelve feet deep. The top had a crevasse of rock at the cliff that hung out over the water perfect for diving. We started a fire from twigs lying around and old stumps found in the creek bed, just below and a few feet from the water. Many of the neighborhood boys came over and we all stripped off with nothing but our birthday suits. The thing to do was to warm by the fire a while then run up onto the cliff, and dive in the windy height and start the process again. Luckily, Mother never knew what we did because we would not be able to sit down if she and Dad found out! Only this swimming hole reigns supreme and it guaranteed the sweetest dreams.

Another childhood activities was fishing in the crawfish holes with a line and pole and a piece of bacon fat. It was fantastic when we caught Red Devils, so rich in red color and twice the taste. Down at the creek, Rock Perch were so plentiful; we attached earthworms on our hooks and they were eager to get on our lines. We dropped them whole in corn meal, and one at a time fried them until golden brown. Coming home, we kicked mushrooms and uprooted them not knowing they were fancy stuff to eat.

As young boys, we were always staging fights. In the woods, we took sticks and fought like knights. Taking our positions, hitting the opponent with the stick, falling down, flinging, and kicking our arms and legs like dying rabbits. At night, the body slept but our hearts never rested.

Living on this prairie became an experience of a lifetime. Seeing the birth of each season as it would unfold to this day haunts the remains left behind in one's mind. The spring educated us about the rebirth of its season and if the days during that season spent at Nail's Crossing are unforgettable. Swimming and fishing on Blue River will always be a highlight in my mind. The spring-fed cold water, even at the hottest times in the summer, was a pleasure every one liked to talk about. The smell of the cottonwood trees and the river were ever present. The river flows and the river bends; I always had a longing to be there. The only exception was you didn't want to get to close to a coiled rattlesnake or the electric eel that you did not want to get on your line.

I remember Mother telling me the men in her family were big on "noodling" on the Blue. The deep holes in the river produce large catfish and they would go back into the holes and hook large fish by hand and bring them home for frying. This was a special technique used only by a select few.

Other summer events were the times spent at old Fort Washita. The days there were a highlight to Mother and always elicited a smile. It always enriched her mind and nourished her soul. She liked the wisteria vines that were always present; the blossoms evoked images of a serene, lovely place. You could see the poignancy in the shadows moving across the flowers that were always in the same spot. We had a lot of our summer events and picnics there.

Looking at the Fort in its present day exposure let your mind wonder back in time the way it was before. Now what we see are the ruins and desolation left behind. There are still a few heavy stone chimneys standing and a few walls built from shell limestone. This is just a little way from the Washita River and I imagine the men that manned the fort could view the river from the outlooks.

Other times we spent at Lake Texoma from the Cumberland Cut to the sandy beaches just down from the Roosevelt Bridge, camping for days and the fishing and swimming were just a few highlights to mention. Surfacing in my intricate thoughts, this was nature in its truest form. Once, walking thru the densely wooded area just off the beaten path by a straggly old hackberry tree, we found a feather from a Red-tailed hawk that was lying on the ground by some patches of snakeroot. The idea came to me to use it for writing a document. With no ink of any kind, I found some Polk berries that were ripe and bright in color, so we squeezed them, put the juice in a glass container, cut the feather for a quill pen, and started writing the Declaration of Independence and this was our political contribution.

It was the beginning of the summer solstice and nights were sizzling and lengthy. A plain, white curtain moved slightly at the window, stirred by a faint breeze that made a vain attempt to alleviate the room's collected heat. The best alternative was to lounge out on the porch in hopes of a breeze or a crescent moon to look upon. The other choice was to gaze at the stars at night and dream of the day I would be mature enough to date a Texas girl and have my own place. That became my continuous focus!

We planted cotton every year. Dad used the Old Farmers Almanac every year to get the planting process started. This book revealed all the signs of when to do everything for farming and preparing the land. Dad broke up the land, turned it under, and then waited for the land to settle before making rows for the seed that we planted. It was always enjoyable to select the seeds for planting and afterwards watching the process begin.

First, the little cotton would sprout and come up, and then it began to leaf and grow larger in size. Next were the squares, the term Dad gave them, which would turn into a bloom later fall off. It would leave a green bole that later would open up and produce raw cotton and this is what we picked or pulled. Dad said the best yields from his land came from the strip of they called Rubber's Valley.

The summer thunderstorms came every year and one evening just before bedtime, I saw the thunderheads building and lighting flashing towards the western sky off in the distance. I didn't think of it much until later in the night. We were awakened by a crash of thunder followed by pelting rain. I kept hearing it thunder and could see it lighting. I knew Daddy was watching because he was scared of tornados and bad storms. Dad told Mother, "I better go out and check the storm." He stayed out for a while and later he came back in the house and he told Mother, "I better go awake the kids." She said, "Okay, but I am not going down in that cellar. I have a phobia of cellars and they generally have spiders and bugs, and I'm afraid of the tree limb's that could fall on the door. I will just sit in the car while you and the kids go down there."

The family got in the car and dad drove us up to Granddad's bomb shelter, which was just up the road. The shelter was round and made of concrete, special materials, and a vent at the top. It was supposed to withstand a bomb blast. It had shelves all around the inside and seating at the very bottom and that's where Granddaddy stored all the home canned vegetables.

Dad opened the door of the shelter and we all started to go inside. I looked up and the storm was directly over us. It was raining, the wind was blowing hard and I heard Dad say it's an electrical storm. He was right; the lighting was flashing continuously and Mother was outside praying in the car. Dad knew it was no use asking mother to come down and he was probably praying too.

The storm lasted for about forty-five minutes and it started to move over us. I kept wondering if mother was okay. Mother always said if the Lord was going to take her, she would be ready whenever it happened! That did not stop me from thinking all kinds of bad things and suddenly, the storm was over and Dad opened the door and growled, looking enormously pleased.

The car and Mother were still there. Relieved, I ran to the door of the car and asked if Mother was okay! She said, "Yes, Son. God takes care of me." I was so thankful for God and my mothers' confidence. The rain kept its steady pace all through the night and when morning came, we awoke, finding the land shedding the falling rain. The creek changed from innocent clear to muddy and the rushing creek was almost out of banks from the forced thrust from the rain. Nature, which invented the process, was doing a good job of maintaining it, as old descriptions of the region testify.

The rainy days were what we always prayed for because that meant we did not have to work in the fields. We longed for the rain to come down slowly and rain for days. This is when we talked Dad into going fishing. That was rare in his books because he always had some excuse not to take us. Now if he accepted, it was a treat, Dad knew all the tricks and just to be with him doing something besides working meant the world to us.

Unrushed and steady, like the rise and fall of the cool water running, I learned to live with natural rhythm. Every year I felt the gravity pull of my inner self wanting the river; going back was like being reacquainted with an old friend. The feel was unapologetic, like escaping into a world of my own. I made the compulsory pilgrimage and it held many pleasures. Occasionally the sweet memory of being a carefree kid made me long for my childhood, if I could only turn back the pages of time.

Kneeling on the riverbank, I picked up smooth stones and skipped them across the top of the water. I continued skipping stones until I became distracted by another amusement of the river. Just a few steps away the southern air is different across a hushed prairie, I shed my shoes and leapt barefoot across the meadow. We enjoyed listening to the frogs, crickets, and night birds that began their praise of summer darkness. In the coolness of the evening when darkness begins the fireflies emerged. Rising slowly, we entered into the world of fireflies in my own naiveté by the twinkling of their nighttime flights revealed their codes by their blinking. They had spent their days in the grasses waiting for the night to come to express their luminous intentions. We spent hours watching and collecting them from the countryside. This landscape has a story because they were firmly entrenched.

I knew all this fun wouldn't last, but in just a short spell the rains would stop and it would be back to work. Cotton had to have continuous care. Plowing the beds and hoeing until the harvest. We also had to hoe the Johnson Grass that seemed to always appear no matter how much you took of its' roots. The only way to get rid of them completely was to pull it during wet times when the ground was softer and you pulled the whole root system.

It was getting later into the year and the hot sun rose over the cotton fields, and the heat waves shimmered above the ground. You could see rows and rows of cotton beginning to open and the fields were turning white in color. The big plump soft white cotton was letting us know that it had done its magic and now it was time for the harvest. When the harvest began, we had the support of the whole family, as well as many of our neighbors around the prairie.

I will always remember, old Indian Jacob Blue Eyes. His tired eyes were kind and his straight, coarse hair sprouted straight up from his scalp. His high, strong cheekbones and square jaw carried his craggy skin with elegance. The expression around his mouth was bemused, as though he had just uttered something. He came every year for the harvesting and could out-work the lot of us. Every year Doc Haney's eighty black field hands, the Reynolds boys, the Allen boys, Mr. Slack and Mr. Wilkerson came, and anyone else that wanted a job.

Processing the cotton was a very hot and sweaty job that included dragging a ten-foot sack and filling it up with cotton to be weighed at the wagons. We then took the cotton to the gin for the ginning process. The days spent at the cotton fields were unforgettable; it was sunrise to sunset and the weather was so hot, steam seemed to rise from the fields with midday heat. Perspiration soaked our shirts and poured off of us like someone was taking a pitcher of water and pouring it on to us. This was a measure of relief because it made it somewhat cooler when the wind blew.

This was summertime ... talking about paying for your raising ... this was definitely the hard way. Strangely enough, no one complained. Everyone had different ideas of what we were going to do with the money we received. For most, it was for the support of the family. Sometimes when we caught Dad away at the gin or out in the field, we would have bole fights, until Kaye would intervene and take on all of us. Kaye found little solace in her career when we failed to fall in line. The summer had been finitely precious and worth saving with peace, goodness, and jollity at the end of the season.

Cotton farming on the twelve-mile prairie became one of the profitable crops for the family every year. Jim told me Granddaddy Newton had told him once that our other granddaddy, Finnis Smith, the one from our mother's side of the family, could beat him at raising cotton but he was better than he was at raising corn and oats. Granddaddy was right, there was a newspaper article given to me by Uncle Walter Smith stating that Bryan County's first bale of cotton ginned at the McElreath gin was in 1933. Mrs. F.C. Smith grew the cotton, four miles west of Kenefick. It weighed 1480 lbs in the seed and ginned out 432 pounds of lint. An offer of eight cents a pound was offered for the bale. The Durant Chamber of Commerce, as the usual prize for the first bale, gave a premium of twenty-five dollars to my grandmother, Mrs. Smith.

From one season to the next were new exciting things like hunting Quail in the winter months. The coveys were plentiful every year. Our thoughts were for rain to come and keep the ground moist to prevent the cracks that would destroy the young fowl from becoming adults. The flush of the birds brings a rush of adrenaline that no other sound in the world can emulate. How can it be, though? How can a bird that is six inches tall and weighs barely a third of a pound incite such devoted passion.

It is easy to understand if you have ever experienced the heart pounding exhilaration of a covey rise of a bobwhite quail on a crisp country morning. Even when I knew it was coming, my heart would still skip a beat with the flurry of buff and brown colors scrambling in front of me. I would try to gain my composure and make a clean shot, but mostly I missed drinking in the glorious moment of the most exciting two seconds in the Oklahoma outdoors.

The seasons also gave us the ducks and geese from Canada that migrated each year and stopped to feed on our winter oats and other feed that we planted. The ducks were also very abundant and sometimes covered our ponds that we dug for watering livestock. It was constantly a shock when we came up the dam of a pond not knowing what to expect next, sometimes it was one are two and other times it would be overwhelming with a hundred or more.

Hunting was always exciting just like the stories told to us when I was a young lad. I was told that in the early years, the diets were venison, squirrel, fish, and corn bread. At the time of my youth, pork held first place; everyone desired fried hog meat which took precedence over all else. Every year in December around the eighth through the fifteenth, it was tradition to pick a hog-killing day. We would do this to have food for the family during the winter months. The process was to set up vats to turn the hog over in scalding hot water to scrap the hair off just after shot with a 22-caliber rifle. After this process, we cut the hogs in half and then quartered them.

Every part of the hog was used for processing, such as brains for hogshead cheese, the intestine for casing for links and sausage and chit lings. Feet were processed for pickled pig's feet. The hams and shoulders were salt and sugar cured and smoked in the smokehouse. The back straps were for bacon and special meats. The skins processed for pork skins, and cracklings. The hams were salt cured that special method of taking a very sharp knife and going into the ham where the joints met and turn it and quarter turn both ways so the salt could fall in and cure the ham. This was the method to cure meats. Every year we killed 13 hogs, twelve for the family and one for comers and goers as the old timers called it.

After the harvest, Dad took us to Durant. We walked the streets down town, looking in the windows of the five and dime shops, and stepped inside since the weather would be cold and almost unbearable. One of the great pleasures of these trips was the sensational smell of the hot roasted cashews in one of the shops. I remember the first taste of those wonderful nuts! I thought I had died and gone to heaven!

The next stop was J.C. Penny's where Dad bought us Levis, shoes, and all the clothes we needed for the year. After the shopping, Dad took us to Red's Café on the Square where Red was serving some of the best burgers in town! After the burgers for lunch, we walked the square and saw a street vendor who later sold us hot tamale's. Other times when we came to town, we stopped by George's Drive In and ordered a steak or a cheeseburger and fries before leaving town.

In this period in time, I started smoking cigarettes and that is when obviously my resentment and rebellion phase kicked in. It was easy trying new things. Another product I tried was Day's Work chewing tobacco. Jim and I had left it under a rock in the corner of the yard and it came a rain that same night and to our amazement it was three time in size. I thought, "Wow, this is great!" Jim and I bit off a big plug and wallowed it around for about ten minutes and that's when I turned a whiter shade of pale and lost it. I remember thinking that I had better leave the tobacco chewing to Uncle Boyd; he could handle it.

Smoking was what I liked best and besides, Daddy smoked and rolled his own. He smoked Prince Albert tobacco from a can and Pall Mall "ready made" as they called them when he went to town. I learned to roll a cigarette just like my dad and he never knew I was stealing his tobacco. So on the other end of the spectrum Jim and I had a code when confined to the house. I thought up this code and called it "latté Mora" it didn't really mean anything, it was just something that came to mind for a code. Every time I spoke the code, Jim would meet me outside for a smoke. I guess Mother never knew because Dad always smoked and she could smell the smoke on his clothes and probably just assumed that was why Jim and I smelled, too.

The throes of adolescence were upon me as I was no longer a child, but not quite grown. Jim and I had been scuffling and he started running from me; this made me angry and I picked up a rock, threw it, and hit Jim in the back. This slowed him down and I caught him, the fight was on. Mother came out of the house and Jim told her what I had done. Mother told me to go and get a switch and I obeyed. I found a switch and brought it to her and she gave me a good thrashing, promising to tell my daddy when he got home. My thinking was that I had been punished enough and I tried to rationalize by sulking in my thoughts.

It was late in the evening when Dad got home and it was obvious I was in for it. Jim just sat there on the sofa and kept smiling because he knew I was going to get it. The first thing Mother did was to tell Daddy about the rock that I threw and hit Jim with. Daddy became angry; I never knew he could get this mad and he said, "Son, get over here and take your punishment. I'm going to cut the blood out of you."

Daddy took out his black leather belt and it popped and snapped when he pulled it through the loops of his pants. He grabbed me by the hand with one hand and starting hitting me with the belt that was in his other hand. The belt kept lift me up with every stroke and the hitting became harder and harder.

Dad started to talking to me trying mostly to help me to see a lot of things I had never experienced or understand about myself and Dad. He was straightforward and an honest man and I knew I could trust him. Therefore, I had no choice except to believe him. Consequently, I had to look at myself, at the foolish thing I had done. He made me look down inside my self, just like he made me look at the things in nature. He made me look down at my anger. He told me that I would never be a man until I learned what anger was supposed to be.

In addition, he explained that I would never be a man until I learned to swallow my pride, come back, and say I was sorry. He said I would never be a man until I learned to live with the people closest to me. "Only takes half a man to be able to live out in nature all by yourself," he said. "I do not doubt that I have done a fair job of teaching you that. Wayne, my boy, now it's time you learned to be a whole man, a complete man."

The next day at school, it was time for Physical Education class so I had to go to the gym to suit out for basketball. While at the lockers and all the guys were changing into our trunks one of them came up to me and said, "What's happened to your legs Newton?" I told them that Daddy gave me a whipping last night. Their response was, "Wow, Newton, you have a mean old man!" I did learn my lesson the hard way and tried to keep my temper to myself from that point on.

Unfortunately, that wasn't the last time. There were many more time because of my rebellious attitude and I can honestly say that I had the monopoly and no one in the family could touch me in that department.

The year was 1962 and I was starting Cobb High School. My teacher was Miss Frances Rambo who taught English. I will always remember one day, I walked into the classroom and she began her quote, "The lightning flashed, the thunder roared, and down the street a Dago passed and from his bosom a knife he drew and cut a banana half into." I never forgot it. The school days were great, especially when I was voted class King and we voted Judith as class Queen. We wore the crowns proudly and were honored with a banquet where they served barbequed black bear.

Despite my parents' protests, I was finally allowed to buy Dad's old 48' Ford sedan with the factory flat head eight motor. It also came with a Delco in-dash radio and completely chromed bumper to bumper. Not too far in the future, I bought a 56" Chevy two door hardtop, with a 283 horsepower automatic engine. It was red on red and beautiful and I started driving it to school. Once I could drive, I would stop by Mr. Olsen's Country Store. The gas wars were on and gas was twenty-five cents for a gallon and Winston cigarettes were about the same price. I filled up for five dollars, bought a pack of cigarettes, a bottle of Coke, and a pack of Planter's Peanuts. I walked out of the store with the bottle of pop, took a drink and it backfired up my nose and man it hurt, but these were the days.

Becoming enthusiastic about cars, my instincts were running wild. My friend, Richard, came over in his Pontiac convertible and took us riding. Conversation was never a prerequisite for friendship as a young man, but adventure was and we liked to go to what we called "thrill hill", this was just north of Durant on a dirt road. Talk about exciting, he accelerated the speed up to about a hundred and the car would leave the ground for a second just after reaching the top of the hill, then come plunging down. We were laughing like crazy men and so excited. Man, it was like your heart would stop beating for a second and then we would regain consciousness. It was like the revival of an old melodrama that I seen long ago with childish awe!

Shortly after this experience, it was on to our group of friends to meet on some dirt road to bring out the bottles of Ever Clear "100 Proof," and challenge each other to a drink. Luckily, this did not happen much because what kept me from over indulging was the thought that always came to mind, "Do you want to end up like your Grandfather Smith?" As well, I remembered what Mother always told me, "Son you better stay out of trouble and watch who you hang around with cause you know your daddy won't come and get you out of Jail." I thought she could see beneath my skin, and worried about me. She is reminding me I can be strong and do the right thing.

Afterwards we rode over to get the girls and rode with the top down in the main drag in Durant. We loved driving the area at the college where all the Magnolia trees grew. The girls would sit all around the back seat of the convertible expressing their vocal cords. Man, we thought we were "big time."

I graduated with the Cobb High School Class of 1966 and soon thereafter, started my college career at Oklahoma State University in 1967. I completed a certificate program and moved to Ft. Worth, Texas, in 1968 where I stayed with my sister, Dretha. I was lucky enough to get a job at General Dynamics and began working on the F111 Defense Project. I was making good money and moved to my own place at Forest Park Boulevard in Ft. Worth.

On July 18, 1968, I got the news that Grandfather had passed away. He was ninety-two and turning my thoughts back to when I first remembered him, it seemed only a short time in my life, but now I caught a glimpse of eternity. The years were a mirage, and that there had been no years. I broke the illusion and set the years moving with a petulant, irritable feeling of my loss.

From time to time, I would go back home and help Dad and my brother Jim with up and coming events on the prairie, like stocking the barns with hay for winter. One time in particular, Dretha and I came up for the weekend. Jim and I, we were hauling hay and after we had moved several loads that day it was getting close to the last load of the day. I decided to ride from the field and back to the barn on top of the hay above the cab of the truck. Jim was driving and we turned on to the highway for a mile or so and when we were exiting the road, Jim had to slam on the brakes to keep from running into an oncoming vehicle. In all this madness, the hay that I was sitting on came off the top and fell and I struck the top of the cab on my left side, hitting my left foot.

My foot was hurting something terrible, but I had a double date planned with Orville and there was no way I missing going out. I got home and dressed for the evening, excited about the blind date that was imminent. In all my pain and excitement, we went to Sherman, Texas to the outdoor drive-in theater for a movie. During all this time my left foot, the weaker one since the polio had turned it slightly to one side, was hurting something terrible. Dretha and I stayed the night and started back home on Sunday. She noticed my painful grimaces and as if I was okay. I replied, "No! I think my foot is broke." She looked at me funny and then drove me to the doctor. I was right, it was broken. This was the trite question answered! Now all this time I had walked on a broken foot, which stayed in a cast for nine weeks.

Just before the accident, I purchased a 66" Chevelle Super Sport with 396 horsepower engine and four in the floor, with a quad stereo and now I could not drive it. I was miserable, but something great was about to happen. Across the street, a friend of Dee's, Evelyn, had some family over for the weekend and out of her house walks this fantastic looking girl, with brown hair and hazel eyes, an attractive body and an awesome smile. Dee had invited her over to her place.

It was destiny and not knowing that this was a set up, I asked her for a date and she accepted. She looked at me with an intensity that obviously came out of deep feelings. This magnificent person was Becky McCaslin. All I could think about was that I had to see more of her and later in the year, Becky and her family moved to Ft. Worth. Becky was not only beautiful, but loved to dance and knew all the newest steps. She also loved music and that was something we had in common. She sang the words to songs that both of us liked. It was then the magic started and I felt her love all around me and knew we had perfect chemistry. After we dated for a while, I went to Oklahoma City to my oldest sister Janelle's home for vacation, it was then I felt the seclusion and at that valley, I knew I was in love with Becky. I couldn't stop thinking about her and though I had a slight fear of commitment, I knew I couldn't be without her.

The enchantment started an amazing relationship between the two of us. I asked for her hand in marriage and she refused the first time, but as our dating increased, we developed a greater attachment which grew into an opportunity to ask again. She accepted and the planning for the wedding began. Originally, we thought about having the wedding on September 12th, which was her birthday. However, the blessed day, which began with a great deal of soul-searching, was August 15, 1970. We were married at White Settlement, Texas by Reverend C.M. Henson who gave us the Rites of Matrimony that was followed by a great reception with all my friends and family, and Becky's attending.

On our wedding night, we checked in the hotel and I was taking care of all the suitcases when Becky asked me to go get her a Coke. She ran into the bathroom and locked the door. I started down the hall to the soda machine and got one and on the way back, I felt in my pocket for the key. I found it and opened the door.

I looked around to see where Becky was and she and her suitcase were in the bathroom with the door locked. I asked if she was okay and she said that she was not coming out. I kept talking to her through the door and she finally came out wearing a negligee and ran and jumped in the bed, and pulled the covers up to her head. I kept asking, "Why are you so shy." She said I had never been in the situation before. I realized that while she loved me, she was young and not sure what to do. I pulled down the cover and looked deeply into her eyes. She said, "I have the feeling you can see right through to my soul!" For a brief moment, the well-timed silence was more eloquent than words, I felt mildly apologetic and she looked slightly embarrassed. I drew a long breath and after seconds of hesitation, associated my self with the situation and slid into bed with her.

Our song was "Love Is All Around Us" by the Troggs and to this day, every time we hear this song, it associates that special meaning of our love for each other. Becky and I liked to cruise downtown Ft. Worth. We also loved attending concerts and some of the ones that we enjoyed were Steppenwolf, The Zombies, and The Beach Boys. Music has always been a part of my family and I remember playing the guitar at age twelve. I had purchased my first Gibson in 1963, along with my Fender Deluxe Reverb Amp, at Wakefield's Music Store in Durant and I was allowed to pay it out monthly. These instruments brought unforgettable sounds to mind and I never turned down a gig!

One month after Becky and I were married, President Nixon cancelled the F111 Defense contract with General Dynamics, which constituted a layoff, and forced me to look for employment. I worked for General Electric in Oklahoma City long enough for another layoff. Then, we moved back to Texas and I started working for Foster & Klaiser in Ft. Worth.

Becky became pregnant and delivered a beautiful baby girl on January 20, 1972. Tracy Renea weighed in at 8 lbs. 4 oz. and was our first baby! Man, was I a happy camper until all the attention went to Tracy and I became the third wheel. I soon came to my senses and took on the hardest thing I have ever encountered and that was being a parent. Tracy's birth started a whole chain of events, first I got a job with Enserch Corporation which at that time was Lone Star Gas Plastic Plant located in Corsicana, Texas. Becky was excited and the move was convenient because this was the town where Becky's mother and family now lived.

Life was going great and Tracy was close to her first birthday party when I got the news that mother was very sick and asked all the children to come. When I arrived, I saw the white chenille bedspread that was on her bed, it was her favorite. She was ashen in color and wearing a simple cotton gown and just barely breathing. I gave her a warm embrace and kept thinking of winters past and how they were always hard on her. It was obvious that this was ending. I felt exhaustion and uncertainty.

All of these complications began to speak to me in abstractions and I remembered her purpose was her greatest privilege. I then felt that genial Spirit about half an hour until she passed away. It was as if she were waiting to say good-bye.

When she died on January 21, 1973, my life changed, Mother meant the world to me and I could not think of giving her up. In the beginning, I believed every word she said and now that she was gone, all I could hear was her voice inside my head! Mother always said men take sorrow harder; especially Daddy whom she would say took strength from her. She told me, "Lloyd always seemed tough. That is not so." Daddy, deep inside, had a soft heart. I could sense his pain. Day after day, it was hard facing life without her and I was continuously aloof.

Then the following months brought about a change that I needed. Becky was pregnant again and on March 11, 1975, another magnificent thing happened. Another daughter was born we named Christie Michele and she weighed in at 9 lbs. 8 oz. She was not like her sister Tracy at all. Christie cried a lot and I could tell she was willful from the start. Man, was I in for it, Christie was insolently a one of a kind who didn't take to the corrective parental configuration. Tracy asked us after being with Christie and all the crying, "Can we take her back?"

Tracy could not wait to go to school, but as soon as she realized Christie would be home, she wanted to go back home and started to cry. We managed to talk her into staying at school. We were surprised she stayed the whole day. From that point on, she was excited to go each day.

Becky had this preconceived idea of owning a Victorian home, but the closest thing I could afford was the home on Winfield Drive in Corsicana. We moved right beside the most wonderful person we called Grandma Crumbly. We all fell in love with her as she was the perfect neighbor and very attentive to the kids. Our neighborhood was filled with great people; across the street were Granny Pat and Johnny, Oren and Lucile, Paulette and David, and T.G. and Agnes. We felt welcome, it was as if our acquaintances shared our destinies, they were overlapping our own. At first, I couldn't tell if Becky was anxious or excited. However, I knew I could not back away from this challenge because we were in this unique situation. My thoughts were of finding the perfect place to raise a family and this seemed the perfect anecdote we were looking for.

Just when things started to settle down and our lives were fairly peaceful, I received horrible news. Daddy was in the hospital and the prognosis was not good. He had been suffering from lung cancer for months now and the tumor had now grown to his heart. I went to see him and as I crouched down by his bed, he had that unmistakable reprimand in his voice. He clenched my hand and asked, "Please have them take the catheter out, it's hurting me and I can't stand it any longer." I asked the nurse what she could do, but there wasn't another alternative. We could not be comforted, except for the words from his nurse just before he passed away. She simply said, "He touched God today."

I was still left with unbridled grief and I was attempting to conceal the tears that didn't go away. It was September 10, 1979, and his death left the family devastated. I remembered the intensity of his words "Remember your legacy, Son." The world did stop that day and time stood still and Old Father Time was good to me that day. I went back in time and viewed my life with Daddy and our life together and what it really meant to me.

Viewing the sky and whispering into the night, I thought, "The call is for you, Daddy." I was looking and not missing a star, wondering which one is you tonight. I can hear the music that you're playing, softly luring me; and the wisdom that you're speaking lets me know you're all right. Will the world ever be the same?" No, I kept repeating trying to decipher what this would all mean for me. Dad had once told me, "Son, the best ideas often come as the result of a roadblock." This was my roadblock but the ideas didn't compute.

Resentment at the loss of my parents swallowed my identity and for awhile, I became enmeshed with it. I was able to slough of my own misconceptions. Each day became predictable and sometimes dull but, I remembered that life's joys lie in adventure. My responses reflected my experiences. The present was valuable and Faith was telling me it is all I have. I gave away my power when the resentment phase kicked in. It was awesome and thrilling when I decided to get free of the resentment and that gave me my power back.

Two years passed and we were blessed with our third daughter in the form of a 9lb. 10 oz. baby girl on February 26, 1981. We named her April Rachael, both the doctor and Becky were fired because he told me this baby was a boy! April was a very good-natured baby and never gave us any trouble, she hardly cried. Tracy and Christie spoiled her with all their creations.

Visions of my children's lives' and my responsibility to them filled my mind. To be trusted with the well being of their souls, an unexpected wave of fear swept over me. Those images are vivid in my mind grasping the numbering of our days; would be stimulating enough to invest in external values. I was trying to see the story in everything. With the purpose of going through my life, with all my senses open and thinking "what if" a thousand times a day?

Life was rare, mysterious, when I almost had the feelings that time has been suspended. The children were wild with joy of being alive. I felt dependence on tomorrow. There was no adequate way to describe it. Frugality proved intoxicating, the more simplified my life became, the happier.

Living in this small town had it own unique set of simple, noncompetitive, restful pleasures to be discovered and enjoyed. We were living in harmony that was consistent with our own beliefs. This became the faith journey of the soul to uncover that longing. These merging ideals became our perfect gift. Becky would say, "Share your enthusiasm with the world around you, for joy is infectious."

When we open ourselves to nature, when we explore the world around us with our feelings and emotions rather than our intellect, we engage all our senses and we invite our children to do the same. The reward was just like my childhood by their joy. I was seized by the strange impulse to say yes. They rose, dripping and triumphant, shouting. We had the first swim of the year! Then they ran home hollering for the thrill of it and to keep from weeping from the cold. The kids kicked off their shoes and opted for bare feet. I guess that was enough nature for one day!

Chapter 5

▼

Our Legacy

Due to the pioneering spirit of those who discovered this prairie, my family has been able to leave a legacy for future generations of a piece of land that still mirrors the wild prairies of yesterday. This leads to uniquely American experiences you won't find anywhere else. Stretch your legs, open your mind and take in the natural beauty of the rhythm of this prairie ... I am about to take you with me on a tour of the prairie.

The prairie landscape is preserved. To love a prairie, you must walk on it. This is an endlessly variable vegetation, not only the native grasses, but wild flowers remnants are a great sweeping generality. This is our history that developed America's habitat of deeply rich organic soil where herds of roaming bison, elk, white-tail deer, mule deer, prairie chickens, quail, and all other species flourished. Looking back, I am proud that my family was a part of this glorious historic past. To survive the challenges that Great Grandfather, who ventured into this remote landscape and survived prairie fires, prolonged summer drought and fierce winter blizzards, faced is something to view in awe. He continued his dream for generations to come and passed on this prairie legacy. It will depend on our consciousness and an outreach effort to keep our actions "alive."

This faithful journey is a montage of seasonal motifs in transition. I became infatuated with the notion of comparing the grassland prairie to the ocean, both flowing in waves and seemingly untouched. I was born with an affinity for the outdoor adventure. The tall grass oriented a one of a kind subtlety. In my youth, it offered challenges and rewards. Surrounded by the sights and sounds of the outdoors, my senses tingled from the stimulation. Through all I saw and felt, I sensed the presence of the One who created everything I was enjoying.

It was like an outdoor overload of reflections of all that I have been blessed to experience, and all of those with whom I shared those times. In the masses of outdoors all around the world, we live in a country that is free and we have the freedom to enjoy these natural encounters. The patina of this heirloom was acquiring that kind of prairie savvy seemed a bit intimidating, especially to novices that came here to dissolve the apprehension.

The reality is I like to look back with enough experience to fondly appreciate and enough drive to still plan and anticipate the future. Maybe it is affirmation that good things do come in their own time. I hope that I can share this experience with anyone that can appreciate it.

The beauty of the prairie is phenomenal; from the land to the sky. Hanging in the tatters of a fading thunderstorm is what must be the biggest rainbow God has painted since Noah's day. Its' colored bands arched thousands of feet over the grassland, challenging a sky that usually laughs at puniness of everything around. My eyes traced the rainbow's right leg to the ground, where it illuminates a lone tree on the horizon.

These surprising rushes of wide-open beauty are waiting just past the Bryan County line. The wind once rustled throughout thousands of acres of tall prairie grass in the future of Indian Territory. Now most of these prairies are gone leaving the memories deep in our hearts.

The journey continues with grace. The pull of earthy passion and the compelling, spiraling course of Blue River in its' balancing acts, transforming one's inner self. The feel is an assessment to one's own body as a river, like a gushing force in the stream coursing outward. The river, with an intellect of its own, transforms its' current with its' own free will to the waters that hold her in submission.

The stream disappears into the forest and hypothetically reappears again and unmistakably finds itself in a small open low place, like Nails Crossing. It was a place where dreams came true. Sometimes it startles you to think how seldom a human foot has been there before you. The woods with their thorny underbrush pressing across the path whip at your face so that you must protect it with your hand.

Evening comes too soon. A breeze tosses the grasses; a thrush chimes from the woods. I could look down at the silvery moonstreams glinting their way from the ridge to that place by the large rock in midstream where I just witnessed an incredible performance of insects, water and fish.

The grasses along the stream poke out shoots and the banks are left bare by cattle; they crumble as the water tears at the curves and washes away the earth around stunted willows. The river is so high that is seems to lift itself out of the riverbed, pushing aside everything in its path! The roar pulses like heartbeats pushing blood through arteries.

Flying insects are a couple of dragonflies along grasses at the high-water mark lie flattened in the mud, inclined as if in a current, driftwood branches and bleached-out twigs are heaped up along the shore. It is immediately obvious that this is more than the usual rural night, where the world is bigger than life. Without a town in sight and the prairie awash in the light of a full autumn moon, I can see a vast landscape around me.

In this pastoral scene which illustrates the overflowing bounty of the season are bundles of hay that were bleached from the sun. Now deeper in view are herds of cattle peacefully grazing in the distance. The bundles became a bountiful buffet that the cattle encircles and seems completely content to be in this place. Walking on a gravel side road and looking at the barbed wire fence, grassy hills roll a way like waves in every direction. The breeze carries an owl's hoots over a knoll.

I sit down in the grass, lean back on an elbow and look through a frame of swaying seed heads as wispy clouds skid across the blue fall sky. This prairie is a shuttered motel for the migrating waterfowl that occasionally stop by while fleeting for a short stay in the oat fields, a display of natural ecology of the prairie. Over the winds steady rush are the welcome of the honking geese and mallards quacking. Even with this intrusion, the loneliness is splendid, the kind earned by patiently accepting nature's pace. Some people, it makes them nervous. Some people find it amazing. To be here is a special experience of solitude and tranquility. If I were to suggest that you should take a walk in the woods at midnight and howl in an attempt to get wild wolves to respond, would your response be, "Let's do it."

As the pace of life accelerates, time, land and the small things become increasingly precious. That allows us to reap the greatest rewards from our efforts. Everything of a practical bent will interest the plan.

When the first chilly morning of the season awakens us from our drowsy summer slumber an excitement begins to stir. The dawn's frost sits heavily on the grass and turns fencing into a string of stars. Was that a scissortail perching in a hundred-year old oak or just the first turning leaf? A cardinal approaches a Bois d' Arc tree that is closing up its' canopy for the winter.

Seasoned trackers, we stand still and squint hard, looking for signs. On a distant ridge, a yellow patch, surrounded by green, glows like a room where the light has been turned on. At last, the truth dawns on us: Autumn is stealing into the country, on schedule, with its entourage of chilly nights. Then the fires of autumn blaze across the prairie; the flame stays in our mind. This is the crossroads of nature and with God's grace to guide its steps. Autumn lulls a tree into a dormant sleep and in its' slumber it dreams in glorious color and God is eavesdropping and making those dreams come true. There's no better season to relish the beauty of nature than in autumn.

Soon the leaves will start cringing and roll up in clenched fists before they actually fall off. The vast green leaves of summer will vanish like a mirage. First there will be weeks of hypnotic colors so sensuous, shrieking and confetti-like that people will travel for many miles just to stare at them a whole season of gem-like leaves.

Soon after the days begin to shorten, a tree reconsiders its' leaves. It hibernates by dropping its leaves, and at the end of autumn, only fragile threads hold the leaves to their stems. Turning leaves stay partly green at first, then reveal splotches of yellow and red as the last chlorophyll gradually breaks down. Dark green seems to stay longest in the veins, outlining and defining bright colors likes the bevels holding stained glass. Camouflage gone, reds and oranges seem to arrive from somewhere, but they were always present, a vivid secret hidden beneath the green plasma of summer.

As with so many of the sensations we adore, leaf colors don't have any special purpose. We've evolved a response to beauty, and fall leaves sizzle with the flames of sunset, sparkle of spring flowers or shuddering pink of a blush. Leaves, flowers, and animals alike change color to adapt to their environment. However, there is no reason for leaves to color so beautifully in the Fall any more than there is for the sky or ocean to be blue.

It is just one of the haphazard marvels the planet dishes out every year. We find the shimmery colors thrilling, and in a sense, they dupe us. Though colored like living things, they signal death and disintegration. In time, they will become fragile and return to dust. They transcend from one beautiful state to another, much as some religions tell us we will. As leaves lose their green life but bloom with urgent colors, the woods grow up mummified. Nature becomes carnal, mute and radiant.

Leaves have always concealed our awkward secrets. Fall the time when leaves fall from the trees, just as spring is when flowers spring up, summer is when we simmer, and winter is when we whine from the cold.

For children, flurrying leaves are just one of the odder figments of nature, like hailstones or snowflakes. They love to plunge into soft, disorderly mattresses of leaves, tunnel through mounds and hurl leaves into the air walking down a lane overhung with trees in the paint splatter of autumn, one forgets about time and death, lost in the sheer delicious spill of color.

A light breeze and the leaves are airborne. They glide and swoop, rocking in invisible cradles. Fluttering from field to field on small whirlwinds or updrafts, swiveling as they go, they are all wing. In time, the leaves depart. First, they turn color and thrill us for weeks on end. They crunch and crackle underfoot. They shush, as children drag their small feet through heaps along the yard. Dark, slimy mats of leaves cling to one's heels after a rain. In leafy mounds, an occasional bulge or ripple signals a field mouse tunneling out of sight. In our disintegrated, thoughts whose outlines remind us how detailed, vibrant and live are the things of this earth, which perish.

Like the presence of my Father that left a legacy of moral fiber, my character was formed here. It's was while performing our daily chores here on this farm. It is where we were educated in the values and lessons of life. I learned about inner strength and determination to continue in the face of disappointment.

It is where I accepted responsibility, and felt the satisfaction of hard work. The hammer mill grinding until way after dark the different steps taken for all the grains properly placed in the bins and nothing taken frivolously.

I remember noises like the rustle of straw under the cow's feet and occasional bawling of a newborn calf. The barn walls had heard the conversation of a lifetime. This is where we worked out life's problems while tending to live stock. This place was where we discussed everyday survival and shared dream about up and coming events. It is where my Dad talked about his expectation of the family. Dad said, "A little arable farm environment never hurt anyone." This experience taught me to rely on myself and not let anyone else decide my fate.

The legacy is the family, the nest in which the soul is born, nurtured, and released into life. Family, a richer memo of sensory experiences, a more deliberate shape to our days, a more conscious appreciation for the moment at hand, a deeper respect for the inner life, weather the inevitable changes find our own rhythm. This is perhaps the greatest legacy we can bestow on our children: the capacity to be enchanted by the quiet gifts of everyday life. I can't think of a better way to spend time than with my family.

CHAPTER 6

▼

GENERATIONS

Historical perspective of George Washington Newton of Mecklenburg County, Virginia.
First Generation to Indian Territory

George Washington Newton

Born December 28, 1845, Mecklenburg County, Virginia

Died October 05, 1939, Ardmore, Oklahoma

Married to Althea Crumply, 1872, Jackson, Mississippi

Died, 1880, Jackson, Mississippi

Children of George and Althea
Second Generation

William Edward Newton

Born Dec 11, 1876, Jackson, Mississippi

Died July 18, 1968, Durant, Oklahoma

Married Della R. Nancy Penny, October 12, 1896, Sherman, Texas

Born September 18, 1875, Knoxville, Tennessee

Died June 10, 1956, Durant, Oklahoma

Children of William and Della are the following fourteen children and descendants:
First child of William and Della
Third Generation

1. George Edward Newton

Born Sept 19, 1897, Indian Territory

Died November 04, 1969, Bakersfield, California

Married Eunice Francis Brake October 31, 1922, Durant, Oklahoma

Born July 09, 1905, Kentucky

Died April 25, 1977, San Diego, California

Children of George and Eunice Newton are following four children and descendants:
Fourth Generation

1. Loye Edward Newton

Born June, 1924, Oklahoma

Died 1986

Married Wilma, 1944, Frederick, Oklahoma

Divorced, 1957, Oklahoma

Deceased

Children of Loye and Wilma Newton
Fifth Generation

1. Glinda Kay Newton

2. Loyd Newton

3. Kenneth Newton

4. James Newton

5. Sue Newton

Eight Grand children

Fourth Generation

2. Chief Sequyah Newton (Chuck)

Born November 19, 1927

Died Feb 24, 2005

Fourth Generation

3. Lattie Jean Newton Hall

Born April 16, 1930

Married David Hall March 11, 1949

Born, 1930, Texas

Children of Jean and David Hall
Fifth Generation

1. Gary L Hall

Born Sept 08, 1950, Frederick, Oklahoma

2. Benny N Hall

Born August 17, 1951

3. Pam L Hall Jackson

Born June 31, 1959

Jean and David have Ten Grandchildren

Twelve Great Grand children

Fourth Generation

4. Louie Marvin Newton

Born November 01, 1932, Nida, Oklahoma

Children of Louie and Angola Newton
Fifth Generation

1. Diane Newton

2. Darlene Newton

3. Sandra Newton

4. Allen Newton

Second child of William and Della
Third Generation

2. Bertha Elizabeth Newton

Born September 30, 1899, Indian Territory

Died June 22, 1979, Oklahoma City, Oklahoma

Burial June 25, 1979, Wapanucka, Johnson County, Oklahoma

Married William Perry Justus September 5, 1915, Wapanucka, Oklahoma

Born August 25, 1891, Alba, Texas

Died October 11, 1964, Wapanucka, Oklahoma

Father James William Justus

Mother Emily Cornella Chaney

The Children of Bertha and Perry Justus are the following twelve children:
Fourth Generation

1. Emma Gertrude Justus

Born November 05, 1916, Coleman, Oklahoma

Died March 23, 1996, Bethany, Oklahoma

Married Clifton McCoy

2. Golda Justus

Born August 24, 1919, Coleman, Oklahoma

3. Violet Della Justus

Born October 16, 1920, Coleman, Oklahoma

Died April 19, 1999

Married Frank McCoy

Second marriage Earl Cox

4. Albert Justus

Born January 15, 1923

5. Odell Vernon Justus

Born July 07, 1924, Coleman, Oklahoma

Married Beatrice Wright

6. Jimmy Leon Justus

Born December 13, 1926, Coleman, Oklahoma

Married Beulah

7. Betty Ila Justus

Born June 01, 1929, Centinel Washataw, Oklahoma

Married Ural Donaldson 1947

8. Otto Avis Justus

Born September 19, 1931, Centinel Washataw, Oklahoma

9. Ruth Justus

Born November 20, 1933, Atoka, Oklahoma

10. Bonnie Glee Justus

Born January 14, 1935, Wapanucka, Oklahoma

Married William Henry Goss October 1952

11. Marland Floy Justus

Born March 01, 1938, Atoka, Oklahoma

Married Dorothy

12. Curtis William Justus

Born February 28, 1941, Atoka, Oklahoma

Died August 08, 1987, Wichita Falls, Texas

Married Eva

Third child of William and Della Newton
Third Generation

3. Zora May Newton

Born May 21, 1902, Indian Territory

Died October 21, 1982, Durant, Oklahoma

Fourth child of William and Della Newton
Third Generation

4. Lora Mamie Newton

Born March 06, 1904, Indian Territory

Died December, 1984, Atoka, Oklahoma

Married October 05, 1919, Earnest Justus Atoka, Oklahoma

Born August 23, 1898

Died October, 1982, Atoka, Oklahoma

Children of Lora and Earnest Justus are the following ten children and descendents:
Fourth Generation

1. Maretta Justus

2. Travis Justus

Born August 15, 1923

Married Erma Dean

Born 1930

3. David Justus

4. Herman Justus

Born July 19, 1921

Died March 28, 2002

5. Lavetta Justus

6. Everett Earnest Justus

Born January 26, 1937

Died June 03, 2003

Married Georgia Lee

Born 1941

7. Elgin James Justus

Born 1939

Married Lois Ann

Born 1941

8. Hershel H Justus

Born 1941

Married Helen R

Born 1949

Second marriage Jewel D

Born 1952

Children of Jewel D Brown first marriage
Fifth generation

1. Roger Dale Brown

Born 1972

2. Angela Michell Brown

Born 1974

Children of Hershel and Jewel Justus
Fifth Generation

1. Aimee Callie Justus

Born 1979

Fourth Generation

9. Dward D Justus

Born 1943

Married Helen R

Born 1949

10. Thyren Clint Justus

Born 1946

Married Patricia Ann

Born 1948

Children of Thyren and Patricia Justus
Fifth Generation

1. Sharla A Justus

Born 1970

2. Clint Justus

Born 1979

Fifth child of William and Della Newton
Third Generation

5. Baby Boy died at birth, 1905, Indian Territory

Sixth child of William and Della Newton

6. Baby boy Louie died after birth, 1906, Indian Territory

Seventh child of William and Della Newton
Third Generation

7. Stella Newton

Born, 1908, Bryan County, Oklahoma

Deceased

Married Elbert Lyday Bryan County, Oklahoma

Born October 23, 1899

Died July, 1967

Children of Stella and Elbert Lyday and descendants:
Fourth Generation

Elbert Mitchell Lyday (Junior)

Born March 20, 1929, Durant, Oklahoma

Died March 13, 1997

Married Verlena Mae Estep September 16, 1947

Born May 13, 1931

Divorced December 1959

Married Dena Lucile Bowers September 19, 1960

Born October 24, 1939

Children of Junior and Verlenia Lyday
Fifth Generation

1. Billy Dale Lyday

Born October 28, 1951

Married Mary Lynn Cross September 27, 1969

Born May 03, 1952

Sixth Generation

1. Cynthia Lynn Lyday

Born April 15, 1970

Married Tommy Joe Dillinger June 03, 1988

Born July 08, 1967

Children of Cynthia and Tommy Dillinger
Seventh Generation

Twin Sons

1. Justin Wyatt Dillinger

Born February 22, 1995

2. Ethan Colt Dillinger

Born February 22, 1995

Sixth Generation

2. Shawn Dale Lyday

Born July 10, 1975

Married Lynetta Patton

Born November 06, 1974

Children of Shawn and Lynetta Lyday
Seventh Generation

1. Bryson Dale Lyday

Born January 11, 2002

2. Braylen James Lyday

Born July 11, 2006

Fifth Generation

2. Danny Mitchell Lyday

Born February 04, 1953

Married Charlotte Ann McDonald September 21, 1974

Born September 17, 1955

Children of Danny and Charlotte Lyday
Sixth Generation

1. Michael Dewayne Lyday

Born March 19, 1975

Married Stacie Marie Sheffield-Williams June 18, 2005

Children of Michael Lyday
Seventh Generation

1. Tanner Cord Lyday

Born October 10, 1996, mother Deana Thompson

2. Jaelin Rhea Lyday

Born March 31, 2004

Children of Stacie by first Marriage

1. Caitlin Marie Williams

Born July 28, 1994

2. Joshua Kale Williams

Born March 19, 2001

Sixth Generation

2. Christopher Brent Lyday

Born May 17, 1977

Married Michelle Margaret Shroyer September 20, 2003

Born May 17, 1977

Children of Christopher and Michelle
Seventh Generation

1. Brendon Slade Lyday

Born July 12, 2006

Children of Junior and Dena Lyday
Fifth Generation

1. David Lynn Lyday

Born October 27, 1961

Married Donnie Marie Stringfellow February 14, 1981

Born June 22, 1965

Children of David and Donnie Lyday

Sixth Generation

1. Daniel Renee Lyday

Born September 10, 1985

Children of Daniel
Seventh Generation

1. Trey Parker Ray Lyday

Born October 06, 2004

Sixth Generation

2. Darren Ray Lyday

Born January 26, 1987

3. Dayly Rochelle Lyday

Born July 29, 1992

4. Dawson Mitchell Lyday

Born March 22, 2000

Eight Child of William and Della Newton
Third Generation

8. Linnie Ruth Newton

Born March 22, 1909, Bryan County, Oklahoma

Died August 15, 1998, Santa Barbara, California

Married Archie Lyday Durant, Oklahoma

Born January 19, 1902

Died September, 1969, Stockton, California

Fourth Generation
Children of Linnie and Archie Lyday

1. Doc Lyday

2. Mary Ruth Lyday

<u>*Ninth Child of William and Della Newton*</u>
Third Generation

9. Floyd Rufus Newton

Born July 15, 1911, Coleman, Oklahoma

Died April 26, 2000, Bakersfield, California

Married Lena Mae Jackson, 1930, Bryan County, Oklahoma

Born August 30, 1913, Mayhew, Mississippi

Died September 29, 2005, Bakersfield, California

Daughter of William Robert Jackson & Annie Lou Blankenship

Children of Floyd and Lena Mae Newton are the following six children and descendants:
First child of Floyd and Lena Mae Newton
Fourth Generation

1. James Floyd Newton

Born October 25, 1931

Deceased

Married Ethel Gladine Pace, August 3, 1949,

Born May 10, 1932

Children of James and Gladine Newton are the following nine children and descendants.
Fifth Generation

1. Nita June Newton

Born June 02, 1950, Bakersfield, California

Deceased

Married Larry McGinnis, Texas

Married Tom Hines, Bakersfield, California

Sixth Generation

1. Lela Beth McGinnis

Born July 02, 1971, Texas

Married John English, Bakersfield, California

Seventh Generation

1. Heather June English

Born October 17, 1988, Bakersfield, California

2. Brooke Skye English

Born August 29, 1991

3. Clayton Storm English

Born December 28, 1993

Seventh Generation

Conner Raven McGinnis

Born September 2007

Sixth Generation

2. Gayla Beth Hines

Born August 10, 1983

Seventh Generation

Chancellor Jkalen Hines

Born November, 2006

Second child of James and Gladine
Fifth Generation

2. Cynthia Ann Newton

Born December 20, 1951, Bakersfield, California

Married Ricky Lynn Franklin

Sixth Generation

1. Melissa Ann Newton

Born September 16, 1970, Bakersfield, California

Seventh Generation

Lauren Cynthia Newton

Born February 22, 1990, Bakersfield, California

Mackenzie Nicole Boles

Born December 20, 1996, Bakersfield, California

Sixth Generation

2. Wendy Newton Newman

Born September 13, 1971, Dallas, Texas

Married A.J. Santiago, Copperas Cove, Texas

Seventh Generation

Andrew Santiago

Born June 04, 1995, Dallas, Texas

Nicole Santiago

Born November 23, 1997, Dallas, Texas

Sixth Generation

3. Crystal Lynn Franklin

Born March 25, 1985, Bakersfield, California

4. Jessica Christine Franklin

Born July 20, 1987, Bakersfield, California

Third child of James and Gladine
Fifth Generation

3. Sandra Kay Newton

Born October 13, 1953, Bakersfield, California

Married Leonard Thomas

Deceased

Married Ronald Dean Davidson, Bakersfield, California

Born April 13, 1950, Bakersfield, California

Children of Sandra and Leonard Thomas
Sixth Generation

1. Leonard Layman Thomas

Born June 26, 1975, Bakersfield, California

Married Julie Ann Marie Mashburn

Born December 11, 1976

Children of Leonard and Julie Thomas
Seventh Generation

1. Macy Rae Thomas

Born June 22, 2005, Bakersfield, California

2. Kilee Rian Thomas

Born June 06, 2007, Bakersfield, California

Sixth Generation

2. Terry Allen Thomas

Born October 14, 1979, Bakersfield, California

Married Carissa Michelle Ruiz

Born April 20, 1978, Bakersfield, California

Children of Terry and Carissa Thomas
Seventh Generation

1. Amberleigh Renee Thomas

Born September 16, 2005, Bakersfield, California

Fourth Child of James and Gladine
Fifth Generation

4. James Floyd Newton

Born February 08, 1955

Married Latonia Gene James

Born October 25, 1959

Sixth Generation

1. Jeffery Don Newton

Born June 28, 1978

Married Melanie April Kallam

Born February 14, 1983

Children of Jeffery and Melanie Newton
Seventh Generation

1. Jeffery Don Newton Jr.

Born July 12, 2005, Graham, North Carolina

Sixth Generation

2. Josh Brandon Newton

Born March 10, 1980

Married Monica Irene Layell

Children of Josh and Monica Newton
Seventh Generation

1. Caleb Skylar Newton

Born July 29, 2002, Graham, North Carolina

2. Evan Matthew Newton

Born August 18, 2004, Graham, North Carolina

Fifth child of James and Gladine
Fifth Generation

5. Michael Ray Newton

Born June 06, 1956, Bakersfield, California

Married Kay Black, Bakersfield, California

Married Karen Robinson, Bakersfield, California

Sixth Generation

1. Michael Ray Newton Jr.

Born January 15, 1981, Bakersfield, California

Married Amanda Crawford

Children of Michael and Amanda Newton
Seventh Generation

1. Michael Ray Newton III

Born September 05, 2002, Bakersfield, California

2. Riley Nichole Newton

Born August 21, 2003, Bakersfield, California

Sixth Generation

2. Luawana Michelle Newton

Born November 21, 1984, Oregon

Married Aaron Dansby

Born, Oregon

Children of Luawana and Aaron Dansby
Seventh Generation

1. Macie Dansby

Born June 11, 2002, Oregon

2. Caleb Dansby

Born May 14, 2004, Oregon

Sixth child of James and Gladine
Fifth Generation

6. Wanda Joyce Newton

Born January 10, 1958, Bakersfield, California

Married Dennis Frase

Divorced

Children of Wanda and Dennis Frase
Sixth Generation

1. Christina Denise Fraze

Born November 15, 1977, Bakersfield, California

Seventh Generation

Kelsey Dinae Fraze

Born January 03, 2006, Bakersfield, California

Sixth Generation

2. Christopher Michael Fraze

Born July 12, 1980

3. Charlotte Michelle Fraze

Born July 12, 1980

Seventh child of James and Gladine
Fifth Generation

7. Ethel Gaylene Newton

Born March 08, 1961

Married Eric Lynn Tritch

Born April 29, 1958

Sixth Generation

1. Matthew Brice Newton

Born November 27, 1986, Bakersfield, California

Seventh Generation

Bryston Eric Newton

Born June 29, 2007, Bakersfield, California

**Eight child of James and Gladine
Fifth Generation**

8. Norma Louise Newton

Born March 13, 1963, Bakersfield, California

Married Lloyd Dwayne Wilson

Born August 21, 1960, Bakersfield, California

Sixth Generation

1. Dawn Gayle Wilson

Born February 10, 1983, Bakersfield, California

2. Amber Leann Wilson

Born June 12, 1985, Bakersfield, California

**Ninth child of James and Gladine
Fifth Generation**

9. Rita Lorraine Newton

Born June 17, 1964

Married Howard Cox

Born February 10, 1963

Sixth Generation

1. Ashley Lorraine Cox

Born May 30, 1984, Bakersfield, California

Seventh Generation

Cameron Xavier Brown

Born May 04, 2004, Bakersfield, California

Sixth Generation

2. Cassandra Rose Cox

Born June 03, 1987

3. Nicole Cox

Born February 26, 1989

Second child of Floyd and Leana Mae Newton
Fourth Generation

2. Billy Ray Newton

Born July 27, 1934

Married Frances Ruth Short, July 10, 1953

Born May 29, 1935

Children of Billy Ray and Frances Newton are the following six children and descendants:
Fifth Generation

1. Bill Dwayne Newton

Born May 03, 1954

Married Debra Ann Wilson August 24, 1974

Children of Bill Dwayne and Debra Newton are the following four children and descendants:
Sixth Generation

1. Kimberly Ann Newton

Born January 06, 1977

Married Brandon Fields

Children of Kimberly and Brandon Fields
Seventh Generation

1. Kailee Cherie Fields

Born April 03, 2007

Sixth Generation

2. Cheryl Lavonne Newton

Born March 26, 1979

Married Weston Blankenship

Children of Cheryl and Weston Blankenship
Seventh Generation

1. Garret Weston Blankenship

Born October 19, 2000

2. Gage Easton Blankenship

Born October 10, 2002

Sixth Generation

3. Stacy Breann (twin)

Born June 21, 1995

4. Tracy Deann (twin)

Born June 21, 1995

Fifth Generation

2. Steven Ray Newton

Born September 20, 1955

Married Linda Kay Griffin September 20, 1980

Children of Steven and Linda Newton are the following four children and descendants:
Sixth Generation

1. Amanda Lynn Newton

Born January 16, 1983

Married Nick Holmes

Children of Amanda and Nick Holmes
Seventh Generation

1. Katelynn Grace Holmes

Born November 03, 2006

Sixth Generation

2. Jennifer Ann Newton

Born June 04, 1984

Married Robert Miller

3. Stephanie Kay Newton

Born May 10, 1987

4. Steven Ray Newton

Born July 03, 1990

Fifth Generation

3. Richard Dennis Newton

Born January 12, 1957

Married Michelle Lee James in June 16, 1978

Children of Richard and Michelle Newton are the following four children and descendents:
Sixth Generation

1. Brent Alan Newton

Born December 01, 1979

Married Shelbi Milam

Children of Brent and Shelbi Newton
Seventh Generation

1. Conner Blanie Newton

Born December 21, 2005

2. Carson Dane Newton

Born April 01, 2007

Sixth Generation

2. Chad Richard Newton

Born April 25, 1982

3. Brian Dennis Newton

Born October 22, 1984

4. Chris Lee Newton

Born November 29, 1986

Fifth Generation

4. Gary Don Newton

Born October 05, 1958

Married Dawn Lynette James October 05, 1979

Children of Gary and Dawn Newton are the following three children:

1. Alyssa Dawnette Newton

Born October 19, 1990

2. Gary Don Newton Jr.

Born December 29, 1991

3. Kara Diane Newton

Born February 13, 1992

Fifth Generation

5. Rita Francine Newton

Born August 17, 1961

Married Carl Danny Black June 15, 1979

Children of Rita and Carl Black are the following two children:
Sixth Generation

1. Carl Danny Black

Born April 10, 1981

2. Valerie Rene Black

Born August 02, 1982

Fifth Generation

6. Randy Lee Newton

Born January 29, 1965

Married Diana June Stanley December 24, 1988

**Children of Randy and Diana Newton are the following four children:
Sixth Generation**

1. Randy Lee Newton

Born October 17, 1988

2. Corine Diann Newton

Born August 28, 1990

3. Lacy Dawn Newton

Born October 05, 1991

4. Cody Ross Newton

Born December 28, 1993

**Third Child of Floyd and Lena Mae Newton
Fourth Generation**

3. Harold Dwayne Newton Nickname "Harry"

Born November 09, 1936, Durant, Bryan County, Oklahoma

Married July 13, 1961, Patsy Ann Kasinger

Born April 02, 1938

Father Art Edward Kasinger

Mother Johnnie Jewel Riggs

**Children of Harold and Patsy Newton the following three children and descendants:
Fifth Generation**

1. Kelly Karen Newton

Born March 26, 1959

Married August, 1988, Mark Vargus, Fresno, California

**Children of Mark and Kelly Vargus
Sixth Generation**

1. Kristen Vargus

Born September 18, 1983

2. Brooke Vargus

Born August 24, 1988

Fifth Generation

2. Suzanne Newton

Born November 28, 1961

Married, Mark Bolen, August, 1980, Bakersfield, California

**Children of Mark and Suzanne Bolen
Sixth Generation**

1. Megan Bolen

Born February 22, 1982

2. Lisa Bolen

Born January 17, 1985

3. Heather Bolen

Born November 18, 1988

Fifth Generation

3. Johathan (John) Dwayne Newton

Born August 08, 1969

Married February 14, 1994, Judi Jost, Lake Tahoe Eldorado County, California

Children of Jonathan and Judi Newton
Sixth Generation

1. Ali Suzanne Newton

Born May 05, 1995

2. Jennifer Lynn Newton

Born May 05, 1995

Fourth child of Floyd and Leana Mae Newton
Fourth Generation

4. Maylene Newton Claborn

Born June 17, 1942, Durant, Oklahoma

Married May 18, 1959, Calvin Ray Claborn Lamont, California

Children of Maylene and Calvin Claborn following three children and descendents:
Fifth Generation

1. Kevin Ray Claborn

Born January 11, 1961, Bakersfield, California

Married June 13, 1998, Andrienne Denise Mayfield

2. Barry Lyn Claborn

Born April 10, 1967, Dinuba, California

Married September 25, 1987, Melanie Janelle Gunn

Children of Barry and Melanie Claborn
Sixth Generation

1. Lucas Shane Claborn

Born July 7, 1991

2. Brennan Taylor Claborn

Born April 29, 1994

3. Jaycie McKenna Claborn

Born August 30, 2002

Fifth Generation

3. Kristina Renee Claborn

Born October 6, 1968, Dinuba, California

Married February 11, 1989, Nathan Paul Morton

Children of Kristina and Nathan Morton
Sixth Generation

1. Drew Claborn Morton

Born July 18, 1990

2. Gentry Paul Morton

Born November 23, 1992

3. Alayna Maray Morton

Born September 10, 1996

Fifth child of Floyd and Lena Mae Newton
Fourth Generation

5. Barbara Jean Newton

Born January 27, 1949, Durant, Oklahoma

Married C. Mel Pearson December 15, 1977

Deceased

Married Kenneth J. Kendrick, February 25, 1995

Children of Barbara and Mel
Fifth Generation

1. Justin Lance Pearson

Born November 09, 1978

Married Irma Granados, November 11, 1997

Children of Justin and Irma
Sixth Generation

1. Breanna Shea Pearson

Born April 30, 1999

2. Nia Monea Pearson

Born July 26, 2000

Fifth Generation

2. Bethany Lenay Pearson

Married November 05, 1998, Christopher Wedgeworth

Divorced

Children of Bethany and Christopher
Sixth Generation

1. Brennan Chandler Wedgeworth

Born May 12 2000

Sixth child of Floyd and Lena Mae Newton
Fourth Generation

6. Betty Gwen Newton

Born October 30, 1954, Bakersfield, California

Married Alvin Dale Young April 19, 1975

Born May 19, 1949

Children of Betty and Alvin Young
Fifth Generation

1. Ricky Dale Young

Born January 28, 1978

Married August 18, 2007, Ashley Nicole Goff

Born September 12, 1986

2. Nicholas Shane Young

Born October 14, 1981

Married January 24, 2004, Kamie Michelle Goff

Born August 16, 1985

Tenth child of William and Della Newton
Third Generation

10. Lloyd Newton

Born December 10, 1914, Bryan County, Oklahoma

Died September 10, 1979, Durant, Oklahoma

Married Thelma Lee Smith December 28, 1935, Durant, Oklahoma

Born April 21, 1916, Kenfic, Oklahoma

Died January 21, 1973, Durant, Oklahoma

The children of Lloyd and Thelma Newton are the following six children and descendents:

First child of Lloyd and Thelma Newton
Fourth Generation

1. Janell Newton

Born January 02, 1937, Durant, Oklahoma

Married Harold Loyd Adams (Bud), 1956, Hugo, Oklahoma

Born August 17, 1933, Mangum, Oklahoma

Died March 14, 2002, Hot Springs, Arkansas

Daughter of Harold's first marriage

Cathy Ann Adams

Born March 03, 1952, Mangum, Oklahoma

Children of Janell and Harold Adams are the following five children and descendants:
Fifth Generation

1. Gary Dean Adams

Born February 07, 1957, Durant, Oklahoma

Married Raelynn Hoover October 05, 1973, Okla. City, Oklahoma

Born January 03, 1957

Divorced 1979

Children of Gary and Raelynn
Sixth Generation

Darrin Keith Adams McCauley

Born January 07, 1974, Oklahoma City, Oklahoma

Married Theresa Flores November 05, 1995

Born August 23, 1963, California

Children of Darrin and Theresa McCauley
Seventh Generation

1. Taylor Reece McCauley

Born June 20, 1997, California

2. Lloyd Christen McCauley

Born May 05, 2003, California

Second child of Gary and Rae Lynn
Sixth Generation

Clinton Wayne Adams McCauley

Born March 07, 1979, Oklahoma City, Oklahoma

Married Amanda Smith

Born September 10, 1980

Children of Clinton and Amanda McCauley
Seventh Generation

1. Madisyn Jo McCauley

Born May 04, 1999, Oklahoma City, Oklahoma

2. Wyatt Anderson McCauley

Born October 14, 2004

Gary Adams second marriage Dari Gerdes 1980, Oklahoma City, Oklahoma

Born April 21, 1956

Divorced 1991

Children of Gary and Dari Adams
Sixth Generation

1. Levi Lyndon Adams

Born August 26, 1981, Oklahoma City, Oklahoma

2. Abby Dee Adams

Born September 14, 1984, Oklahoma City, Oklahoma

Gary Adams third marriage on February 14, 1992, to Victoria Wells at Bethany, Oklahoma

Born April 07, 1957

Daughter of Victoria Wells

Tori Allison Wells

Born March 11, 1981

Married Jeremiah Burnett May 22, 2004

Born June 09, 1981

Second child of Janell and Harold Adams
Fifth Generation

2. Barry Neal Adams

Born August 11, 1962, Durant, Oklahoma

First Marriage to Dianne Lytle, 1995, Hot Springs, Arkansas

Second Marriage Judy Czerniak Dragon October 07, 1995, Pearcy, Arkansas

Born, Wisconsin

Children of Judy Czerniak First Marriage

1. Shane Dragon

Born March 9, 1988, Hot Springs, Arkansas

2. Jared Dragon

Born September 15, 1989, Hot Springs, Arkansas

Children of Jared Dragon
Seventh Generation

Breanne Dragon

Born September 26, 2006, Hot Springs, Arkansas

First child of Berry and Judy Adams
Sixth Generation

1. Durant Al Adams

Born May 07, 1997, Hot Springs, Arkansas

Third child of Janell and Harold Adams
Fifth Generation

3. Randy Lane Adams

Born March 4, 1965, Durant, Oklahoma

Married Tammy Morgan June, 1991, Star City, Arkansas

Born Feb 24, 1965, Star City, Arkansas

Children of Randy and Tammy
Sixth Generation

1. Tommy Lane Adams

Born December 13, 1994, Hot Springs, Arkansas

Fourth child of Janell and Harold Adams
Fifth Generation

4. Bart Darrin Adams

Born August 16, 1966, Durant, Oklahoma

Fifth child of Janell and Harold Adams
Fifth Generation

5. Pamela Kaye Adams

Born November 30, 1970, Oklahoma City, Oklahoma

Married Hank Meeks January 27, 1995, Hot Springs, Arkansas

Born Oct 30, 1972

Children of Pamela and Hank
Sixth Generation

1. Alexis Nicole Meeks

Born April 10, 1994, Hot Springs, Arkansas

2. Dustin William Meeks

Born August 29, 2001, Hot Springs, Arkansas

Second child of Lloyd and Thelma Newton
Fourth Generation

2. Dretha Pauline Newton

Born March 02, 1940, Durant, Oklahoma

Married November 4, 1956, Harold Banker

Divorced

Re-married December 02, 1980, Gene Goodwin Poteau Oklahoma

Born April 03, 1931, Chicago, Illinois

Children of Dretha and Harold Banker are the following three children and descendants:
Fifth Generation

1. Dayne Banker

Born June 27, 1959, Durant, Oklahoma

Married Cheryl Newkirk Durant, Oklahoma

Born January 18, 1963

Children of Dayne and Cheryl
Sixth Generation

Amanda Michelle Banker

Born January 06, 1981

Children of Amanda

Seventh Generation

1. Alison Page

Born August 03, 1998, Hot Springs, Arkansas

2. McKenzie Brook

Born June 18, 2004

Second child of Dretha and Harold Banker
Fifth Generation

1. Dena Charlene Banker

Born January 11, 1962, Oklahoma City, Oklahoma

Married Danny Almond

Born April 22, 1944

Children of Dena and Danny
Sixth Generation

1. Brandon Almond

Born July 23, 1981

Second Marriage Bobby Danuser

Born May 06, 1964

Children of Dena and Bobby Danuser

1. Sidney Shay Danuser

Born March 06, 1988

Third child of Dretha and Harold Banker
Fifth Generation

2. Cheri Denise Banker

Born, July 18, 1962, Ft. Worth Texas

Married Joe Gamble

Born February 23, 1967

Child of Cheri and Joe Gamble
Sixth Generation

1. **Amber Cheri (Stillborn)**

Children of Cheri and Danny Mosley

Sixth Generation

2. Clayton Mosley

Born February 14, 1993

Cheri Married Danny Dickey Hot Springs, Arkansas

Children of Cheri and Danny Dickey

Twin Daughter's

1. Destiny Dickey

Born December 09, 1999 Hot Springs, Arkansas

2. Danielle Dickey

Born December 09, 1999, Hot Springs, Arkansas

Third child of Lloyd and Thelma Newton
Fourth Generation

3. Linda Kaye Newton

Born April 20, 1944, Durant, Oklahoma

Married Don Holland November 20, 1975, Hot Springs, Arkansas

Born February 05, 1938, Hot Springs, Arkansas

Children of Linda and Don Holland
Fifth Generation

1. Shon Holland

Born July 10, 1973, Hot Springs, Arkansas

Fourth child of Lloyd and Thelma Newton
Fourth Generation

4. Loyd Wayne Newton

Born August 04, 1948, Durant, Oklahoma

Married Becky McCaslin August 15, 1970, White Settlement, Texas

Born September 12, 1954, Corsicana, Texas

Children of Loyd Wayne and Becky Newton are the following three children and descendents:
Fifth Generation

1. Tracy Renae Newton

Born January 20, 1972, Weatherford, Texas

Married Michelle Rozelle October 26, 1991, Corsicana, Texas

Born September 18, 1971, Dallas, Texas

Children of Tracy and Michael Rozelle
Sixth Generation

1. Chloe Elizabeth Rozelle

Born January 08, 2000, Plano, Texas

2. Sarah Nichole Rozelle

Born August 04, 2003, Allen, Texas

Second child of Loyd Wayne and Becky Newton
Fifth Generation

2. Christie Michele Newton

Born March 11, 1975, Corsicana, Texas

Married Adam Strickland August 2, 1997, McKinney, Texas

Born January 05, 1968, Dallas, Texas

Children of Christie and Adam Strickland
Sixth Generation

1. Noah Reid Strickland

Born August 22, 2001, Plano, Texas

2. Caleb Cole Strickland

Born May 29, 2007, Allen, Texas

Third child of Loyd Wayne and Becky Newton
Fifth Generation

3. April Rachael Newton

Born February 26, 1981, Corsicana, Texas

Married Chad Butler July 05, 2003, Denton, Texas

Born April 02, 1979, Dallas, Texas

Children of April and Chad Butler

Sixth Generation

1. Lauren Ashton Butler

Born May 10, 2006, Allen, Texas

2. Katherine Leah (Kate)

Born October 02, 2007, Allen, Texas

Fifth child of Loyd and Thelma
Fourth Generation

5. Jimmy Harold Newton

Born December 08, 1950, Durant, Oklahoma

Married Sharon Risner October 10, 1969, Durant, Oklahoma

Born February 16, 1949, Durant, Oklahoma

Deceased

Daughter of Inell and Murell Risner

Children of Jimmy and Sharon Newton are the following two children and descendants:
First children of Jimmy and Sharon Newton
Fifth Generation

1. Timmy Shane Newton

Born July 04, 1970, Durant, Oklahoma

Married Christy Marshberry in Durant, Oklahoma

Born 1970

Children of Timmy and Christy Newton
Sixth Generation

1. Madison Newton

Born March 03, 1990, Durant, Oklahoma

2. Riley Newton

Born February 23, 1996, Durant, Oklahoma

Second child of Jimmy and Sharon Newton
Fifth Generation

2. Tara Shanell Newton

Born December 10, 1976, Durant, Oklahoma

Married Travis Stephens

Children of Tara and Travis Stephens
Sixth Generation

1. Colton Ray Stephens

Born November 11, 1994, Durant, Oklahoma

2. Cooper Shane Stephens

Born March 21, 1997, Durant, Oklahoma

3. Colby Lane Stephens

Born May 11, 1999, Durant, Oklahoma

Second marriage April 14, 2005

Bradley Wayne Sharp

Born March 03, 1967, Sherman, Texas

Father Jacky Sharp

Mother Anna Jay Sharp

Children of Bradley Sharp

1. Brittany Ann Sharp

Born March 31, 1988

2. Logan Briann Sharp

Born September 14, 1993

Sixth child of Loyd and Thelma Newton
Fourth Generation

6. Sharon Elaine Newton

Born December 02, 1953, Durant, Oklahoma

Married Melvin Brown February 15, 1973, Durant, Oklahoma

Born February 03, 1947, Roswell, New Mexico

Second marriage April 01, 1995, Hot Springs, Arkansas

Donald Slater

Born March 02, 1953, Denver, Colorado

Children of Elaine and Melvin Brown are the following three children and descendants:
Fifth Generation

1. Nathan Lee Brown

Born September 25, 1975, Durant, Oklahoma

2. Justin Lane Brown

Born July 15, 1980, Durant, Oklahoma

Married Amy Cheshier

Born December 03, 1983

Children of Justin and Amy
Sixth Generation

1. Justin Lane Brown Jr

Born May 24, 2005, Hot Springs, Arkansas

2. Lilly Ann Brown

Born May 09, 2006, Hot Springs, Arkansas

Fifth Generation

3. Crystal Janell Brown

Born September 15, 1983, Ada, Oklahoma

Eleventh child of William and Della Newton
Third Generation

11. Beulah Ester Newton

Born April 30, 1917, Bryan County, Oklahoma

Died May 07, 2002, Bakersfield, California

Married Burlin Richardson in 1935, Durant, Oklahoma

Born April 28, 1914, Emit Johnston County, Oklahoma

Died January 21, 1986, Bakersfield, California

Twelfth child of William and Della Newton
Third Generation

12. Velia Lillian Newton

Born May 18, 1920, Bryan County, Oklahoma

Died June, 1967, Stinnett, Texas

Married Perry Studdard

Children of Velia and Perry Studdard

Fourth Generation

1. Shirley Ann Studdard

Born June 04, 1940, Bryan County, Oklahoma

Married William Redden June 29, 1962, Borger, Texas

Shirley second marriage to John Ross August 25, 1970, Lubbock, Texas

Children of Shirley and John Ross
Fifth Generation

1. Brandon Ross

Born November 29, 1975, Lubbock, Texas

Married Tammy Green Lubbock, Texas

Children of Tammy Green

1. Ashlee Green

Children of Brandon and Tammy Ross
Sixth Generation

1. Jade Alexandra Ross

Born April 26, 2006

Velia second marriage to Ernest (Bud) Allen, 1948, Durant, Oklahoma

Born March 13, 1908

Died January 30, 1996, Lubbock, Texas

Bud's Mother and father were Martha and George Allen

Children of Velia and Bud Allen
Fourth Generation

1. Patsy Dianna Allen

Born May 22, 1949, Borger, Texas

Married David Sharbutt February 13, 1971

Children of Patsy and David Sharbutt are the following three children and descendents:
Fifth Generation

1. Christina Annette Sharbutt

Born May 18, 1974, San Antonio, Texas

Married Brent McCutchin April 25, 1998

Children of Christina and Brent Sharbutt
Sixth Generation

1. Madalyn Ann McCutchin Answers to the name Maddy

Born January 20, 2002, New York City, New York

2. Ella Grace McCutchin

Born December 09, 2003, Austin, Texas

3. Luke McCutchin

Born March 20, 2006, Austin, Texas

Fifth Generation

2. Justin Allen Sharbutt

Born June 21, 1983, Lubbock, Texas

3. Amanda Jeanette Sharbutt

Born September 18, 1985

<u>**Thirteenth child of William and Della Newton**</u>
Third Generation

13. Boyd Willy Newton

Born March 15, 1922, Bryan County, Oklahoma

Married BB La Rue Human January 31, 1947, Sherman, Texas

Born September 27, 1931, Durant, Oklahoma

Children of Boyd and BB Newton are the following five children and descendents:
Fourth Generation

1. Anna Jolene Newton

Born February 29, 1948, Durant, Oklahoma

Married Robert Duane Richardson I

Born September 14, 1970, Cedar Rapids, Iowa

Second Marriage Joe Chesnut November 30, 2002

Children of Jolene and Robert Richardson
Fifth Generation

1. Robert Duane Richardson II

Born July 26, 1971, Lawton, Oklahoma

Married Jennifer Denk November 25, 2000

Children of Robert and Jennifer
Sixth Generation

1. Brandon Duane Richardson

Born July 07, 1989, Cedar Rapids, Iowa

2. James Michael Richardson

Born January 20, 1992, Cedar Rapids, Iowa

Second child of Jolene and Robert Richardson
Fifth Generation

2. Willis Allen Richardson

Born November 03, 1975, Durant, Oklahoma

Married Edwina Proctor September 13, 2003

Children of Willis and Edwina Richardson
Sixth Generation

First child Kristen Leann Richardson

Born July 18, 1995

Third child of Jolene and Robert Richardson
Fifth Generation

3. Shanna Jolene Richardson

Born November May 08, 1977, Denison, Texas

Children of Shauna Richardson
Sixth Generation

1. Jaxon Alan Richardson

Born August 23, 2004

Second child of Boyd and BB Newton
Fourth Generation

2. Lola May Newton

Born December 19, 1949, Durant, Oklahoma

Married Larry Don Haddock May 24, 1968, Bryan County, Oklahoma

Children of Lola and Larry Haddock
Fifth Generation

1. Jimmy Don Haddock

Born July 26, 1969, Durant, Oklahoma

Died July 26, 1969, Durant, Oklahoma

Second Marriage Odis Glen Lamar October 28, 1972

Born April 22, 1939, Durant, Oklahoma

Died July 03, 1998, Denison, Texas

Third Marriage Billy Dwayne Gresham May 24, 2003

Children of Otis Lamar
Fifth Generation

Step son Odis Mearl Lamar

Born October 28, 1962, Durant, Oklahoma

Married Lavonda Gail Nazworth July 18, 1986

Children of Odis Mearl and Lavonda Lamar
Sixth Generation

1. Lyndsey Danielle Lamar

Born March 17, 1992

2. Logan Cheyenne Lamar

Born November 07, 1996, Durant, Oklahoma

First Step daughter of Billy Gresham

Fifth Generation

1. Rosanna Laverne Gresham

Born January 30, 1988

Second step daughter of Billy Gresham

2. Monique Shantell Gresham

Born January 10, 1991

**Third child of Boyd and BB Newton
Fourth Generation**

3. Carolyn Joy Newton

Born March 14, 1953, Durant, Oklahoma

Married Albert William Kelso September 23, 1972, Bryan County, Oklahoma

**Children of Carolyn and Albert Kelso
Fifth Generation**

1. Baby Kelso

Born December 08, 1976, Durant, Oklahoma

Died December 08, 1976, Durant, Oklahoma

Second child of Carolyn and Albert

2. Amanda Joy Kelso

Born November 05, 1980, adopted

**Fourth child of Boyd and BB Newton
Fourth Generation**

4. Kathy LaRue Newton

Born March 22, 1955, Durant, Oklahoma

Married James Lyndel Brister I December 17, 1971, Durant, Oklahoma

**First child of Kathy and James Brister
Fifth Generation**

1. James Lyndel Brister II

Born June 25, 1972

Married Shawna Strickland March 17, 2004

Second child of Kathy and James Brister

2. Boyd Ray Brister

Born May 24, 1974, Durant, Oklahoma

Fifth child of Boyd and BB Newton
Fourth Generation

5. Boyd Lynn Newton

Born January 29, 1957, Durant, Oklahoma

Married Neta Jeffcoat March 28, 1974, Durant, Oklahoma

Second Marriage Melody Kimberly Hansen March 27, 1999, Denison, Texas

Children of Boyd Lynn and Nita Newton
Fifth Generation

1. Lucrita Lynn Newton

Born March 18, 1975, Denison, Texas

Fourteenth child of William and Della Newton
Third Generation

14. Lola Marie Newton

Born October 07, 1923, Bryan County, Oklahoma

Died July 26, 2001, Madill, Oklahoma

Married Doyle Chasteen Allen

Born November 03, 1920

Died June 25, 1988

Children of Lola Marie and Doyle Allen
Fourth Generation

1. Louie Chasteen Allen

Born April 26, 1944, Littlefield, Texas

Married Rhonda Gail Rains

Born October 12, 1947

**Children of Louie and Rhonda Allen
Fifth Generation**

1. Scotty Dean Allen

Born January 06, 1967, Durant, Oklahoma

Married Carla

2. Brian Lee Allen

Born October 24, 1970, Durant, Oklahoma

Married Angela

Grandchildren

1. Blake Austin Allen

Born September 30, 1991

2. Brock Allen

3. Kaily Allen

Born November 19, 1991

4. Branden Wayne Allen

Born May 04, 1999

5. Bailee Lashay Allen

Born January 15, 2001

Second Marriage Johnny Paul Gardner

Born August 25, 1923

Married May 09, 1950

Died March 17, 2000

First child of Lola Marie and Johnny Gardner
Fourth Generation

1. Brenda Gardner Weatherbee

Born March 07, 1951, Durant, Oklahoma

Married June 18, 1987, Charles William Weatherbee Jr. (Bill)

Born September 15, 1940, Ft. Lauderdale, Florida

Mother Janie Sue Peek

Born September 12, 1922, Booneville, Mississippi

Married, 1939

Died June, 1986

Father Charles William Weatherbee Sr.

Born May 09, 1918, Mississippi

Married, 1939

Died May 01, 2006

Children of Brenda Gardner
Fifth Generation

1. Jeffery Don Pilkington

Born June 06, 1969, Durant, Oklahoma

Married Gisela Cadena September 14, 2002

Born January 01, 1979, Crystal City, Texas

2. Matthew Eric Pilkington

Born May 30, 1972

Married Kimberly Brooke Chandler May 03, 2004

Born July 16, 1982, Comer Georgia

Children of Brenda and "Bill" Weatherbee

1. Step-son Chad William Weatherbee

Born July 29, 1965, Coldwater, Kansas

Married Shannon Coffman January 31, 1992, Durant, Oklahoma

Born February 14, 1972, Oklahoma

2. Step-daughter Charlann (Weatherbee) Forguson

Born January 21, 1972, Ardmore, Oklahoma

Married Anthony Forguson June 04, 1994

Born October 08, 1968, Oklahoma

Grandchildren of Brenda Gardner Weatherbee
Sixth Generation

1. Genesis Maleni Pilkington

Born May 12, 2004, Uvalde, Texas

2. Eragon Emanuel Pilkington

Born January 27, 2006, Uvalde, Texas

3. Ocean Brooke Pilkington

Born October 11, 1997, Auburn, Indiana

4. Cole Michael Weatherbee

Born June 27, 1993, Durant, Oklahoma

5. Presley Ireland Weatherbee

Born April 08, 1996, Durant, Oklahoma

6. Kara Kaye Forguson

Born November 08, 1994, Ada, Oklahoma

7. Daylan Wayne Forguson

Born May 23, 1996, Madill, Oklahoma

Second Child of Lola Marie and Doyle Allen
Fourth Generation

2. Lannie Doyle Allen

Born September 16, 1957, Durant, Oklahoma

Children of Lanny Allen

Fifth Generation

1. Jennifer Michelle Allen

Born January 02, 1976, Denison, Texas

2. Anthony David Allen

Born July 07, 1980

3. Luke Douglas Allen

Born January 14, 1986, Durant, Oklahoma

4. Leslie D'Anne Allen

Born July 27, 1987, Durant, Oklahoma

Grandchildren

1. Clayton Paul Russell

Born April 02, 1998, Durant, Oklahoma

2. Chloie Paige Russell

Born September 08, 2003, Durant, Oklahoma

3. Son of Anthony

4. Daughter of Anthony

Third child of Lola Marie and Doyle Allen
Fourth Generation

3. Larry Edward Allen

Born January 12, 1959, Durant, Oklahoma

Children of Larry Allen
Fifth Generation

1. Dianna Marie Allen

Born October 25, 1977

2. Kami Allen

Born January 22, 1981

3. Corey Allen

Born February 16, 1982

4. Joey Dee Allen

Born January 02, 1984

Married Staci Spears

5. Jake Wayne Allen

Born September 01, 1992

Grandchildren

1. Son of Dianna

2. Daughter of Dianna

3. Jory Allen

Born April, 2007

Chapter 7

Reminiscences, Poetry and Songs

When I first began gathering my thoughts on what I hoped to achieve with this book, one aspiration was to make sure my dates and names were as accurate as possible. Therefore, I contacted any and all family members I could, and began my collection of information. Miraculously, what emerged from all of my family's involvement and hard work is Chapter 6, *Generations,* a chapter that is very dear to my heart as it is the most complete compilation of my family's genealogy that I am aware of. However, names and dates were not all my family contributed. As I spoke with each of them, many were eager to tell or write down their own treasured recollections of Twelve Mile Prairie and its inhabitants. I will always be thankful to my many family members who showed so much love and enthusiasm towards my goal of completing this family tale. In appreciation, I wanted to print their many stories, songs, and poems that they so kindly lent me. I have printed these contributions word for word as they came from their respective authors. I hope you enjoy.

A Short Remembrance of my Mother's Family
By Loyd Wayne Newton

One of my greatest regrets is the fact that I never had the privilege of knowing my Grandfather and Grandmother Smith. They passed away before my existence. The only memories are the short stories told to me by my mother in my youth. The information is limited but just as much apart of my legacy.

Finnis Clinton Smith, my Grandfather, was born March 15, 1892, to William Ely Smith and Esther Webb. Finnis married Ellen Webb, who was born March 03, 1891, and died June 23, 1920, in Kenfic, Oklahoma. Ellen was the daughter of Henry Webb, born in 1861 and died 1934 and her mother was Mary Tips born, 1896, and died 1933.

Finnis Smith was father to Ruby Smith born, 1914, and Thelma Lee Smith (my mother) born April 21, 1916, in Kenfic, Oklahoma. A son, Walter Smith was born in, 1925. Two daughters born later were Pearl and Mildred.

Third Generation Remembers Twelve-Mile Prairie
By Walter Smith
Memories of My Life on Twelve-Mile Prairie

At four years old we lived at a place called Nails Crossing on the Blue River. I was my mother's first child, and my sister Opal died at home in 1925. There were three other children born to my mother, Mildred, Pearl and Johnnie Bell who died at childbirth along with my mother, Edith.

My father, Finis, was previously married to Ellen, who had one child from a prior marriage-she and my Dad had two daughters, Ruby and Thelma.

Things had to be pretty tough for Ruby and Thelma being raised from young childhood by two different stepmothers.

Most of my memories of Ruby and Thelma begin about, 1929, when I was eight years old. We lived approximately quarter of a mile from Goodman School house. Our living conditions were very poor but we did not realize it since most families were in the same situation. I picked and chopped cotton along with Ruby and Thelma. A lot of times before school in the morning and pulled up Johnson grass by the roots at the front of cotton rows along the road if it was too wet to chop cotton.

When we gathered corn in the fall I usually drove the mules and wagons, my Dad gather two rows on one side, Ruby took the other two rows and Thelma being the youngest took the down row.

Thelma and I were always at each other for one thing or another ... so this was my opportunity to get even with her for past things she had upset me about. I would purposefully drive the mules up quite a distance so she had would have to throw the corn a long way, but when she did catch up I would need to get under the scoop board to dodge her throwing.

When our Dad ever left the farm to go somewhere, Thelma and Ruby would usually lock me up in the storm cellar to keep me out of their way until it was about time for Dad to get home.

The Devault family was our closest neighbor. Thelma and Ruby spent a lot of time their two daughters, Juanita and Dutch. I hung around with James "Fuzz" was his nickname.

One day, the four girls were down at the barn and didn't want me around so I was curious as to what they were up to. I was down below in the mules stall listening and they were up in the hayloft ... suddenly "water" went to dripping on my head so I left for the house upset.

Shortly after our dad's accidental death in, 1933. Ruby and Thelma were left alone to handle their own lives. Mildred, pearl, and I were sent off to Whitaker State Orphanage. I left there in, 1938. Not long after that I found myself living with Thelma, Lloyd and their young daughter Janelle.

I will always be appreciative and never forgot how Lloyd and Thelma took me in to their little home near Brown, and treated me as part of the of their family. Lloyd was struggling to make a living with the W.P.A. and he let me use his one horse and plow to cultivate a small parcel of land he had for corn and vegetables.

Our early entertainment, which I am sure Lloyd, along with me, enjoyed was sitting close to a small battery, operated radio listening to Lum & Abner. There were times when there was no money to buy a new battery. Lloyd would get out the old guitar, even though there was a string missing, and show me how to play the guitar.

Shortly after that we moved from Brown to a little house on his old home place. Lloyd needed a barn for his cow while he handled his W.P.A. job I gathered poles from the woods around his Dads farm and built a pole barn.

While there with Thelma and Lloyd I met Lloyd's sister, Marie, and even though I was to bashful to even talk to her, I wanted to buy her a birthday present and had to ask Thelma if she had some money to let me have. She had no money but said I could take one the chickens to Durant and sell it. When I got to town I signed up for a door prize at one of the stores and won $5.00. More money that I ever had my hands on so Marie was a recipient of a beautiful comb and brush set for her birthday.

One of my regrets in life is due partially to my families' travels. We lost close contact with Lloyd and Thelma's family and never watched their children grow up. But my family is so grateful that we have had the opportunity recently to get reacquainted with the Newton family and are so impressed with how Thelma and Lloyd's children have grown and their love and closeness to each other and the people around them. I am sure Thelma and Lloyd would be extremely proud of them today.

Their brother Walter Smith

Fourth Generation Remembers Twelve-Mile Prairie
Janelle Newton Adams
Memories of Twelve-Mile Prairie

One of the first things I can remember as a little girl and growing up on twelve-mile prairie was starting the first grade. I went to school at Cobb Grade School. Mrs. James was my first grade teacher. I completed grade school, Jr. High, and High School and graduated in, 1955.

My life on twelve-mile prairie was very exciting. My dad share crop with my Grand Pa Newton.

It was a very busy life my sister Dretha and I would work in the fields all summer hoeing corn and cotton. We also helped Aunt Zora and Aunt Marie hoe grand Pa's, cotton and pick and gather the crops. There was so much hard work for everyone.

My life here on this prairie meant many things to me first was responsibility and caring for others and loving my family and the most important thing. I was taken to church and taught to love Jesus.

Dad would take us to church every Saturday night; and after church would treat us. We never got many extras like candy or soda pops during the week. On Saturday night after church Dad would stop at Lee's service station north of town. Dad would get each of us a Pepsi cola and a large bag of cheetos and a bag of Fritos. We were all so happy going home laughing and eating and drinking those were the good ole days.

We had the most wonderful parents. I wouldn't trade anything for my up bringing, and the life I had on twelve-mile prairie.

Another exciting time I, can remember was the year Dad, made a good cotton crop. It was early in the morning when Dad started for town but before he left he said "Girl's I'm going to buy a new car today." All day long we kept looking down the road to see what kind of car, Dad was bringing home. It was so exciting because we didn't have a car. If we got go anywhere we, would have to walk, or catch a ride with someone else. Well very late that evening, we saw a car coming sure enough it was Dad, driving the prettiest black car, we had ever seen. It was a, 1940, ford. From then on we were so proud to get to go places, with all the family especially we would get to go to church.

Our mother was sick most of her life. She taught all the children to fear the Lord. She never complained about being sick. She Loved God and served him all her life. She was true to what she believed no matter what other people said about her. She was a great light to her community and family. She always stood up for Jesus and loved him with all her heart. She went to be with Jesus on January 21, 1973.

Our Dad was a very special person he worked hard all his life. He was the jolliest person I have ever known always laughing and cutting up with everyone. Everyone loved to be around him especially all the Grand children. They all loved him so much he, was special to them. In the wintertime in the evening all of us children would love it when Dad got his Guitar and Harmonica and play for us. We would make a game out of what dad was playing and guess what he was playing. Our Dad was the best Harmonica player in our community. He played the Train Song, the fox and the hound, the ole hen cackling and many more.

He would play Gospels songs on his Guitar, and harmonica and sometimes he played them at the same time.

Our family loved music, when I would get around a piano, and I just had to touch the keys. When I was about 10 or 11 years old Mom and Dad bought us a piano. Mom sold hen eggs to give me lessons. I took a few lessons and decided I wanted to play different than the music teacher was teaching. I started playing by ear that was the way our Dad played music.

I was playing pretty good when our pastor rev Lee South, started letting me play at church with all the other young girls that was just learning to play. Playing the piano or keyboards is my gig today. All my sisters and brothers can play either the piano or the guitar or the bass.

Since Mom and Dad are gone to be with the Lord. We still are a very close family. Sometimes we still get together and we all have to sing and play together just for ole times like on twelve-mile prairie.

Fourth Generation Continues
Memories
By Shirley Studdard Ross

I have a lot of good memories the years I lived and visited with my grandparents and my Aunt Zora.

My first six years I lived with Grandma and Grandpa Newton and my Aunt Zora on their farm. Part of that time my cousin, Louie, "Butch" to the family, lived there also.

The newspaper came by mail once a week. The day the paper came Grandma was so engrossed in the "news" that she would not pay any attention to Butch and myself. So—one day we grabbed the paper out of her hands "she always sat in her rocking chair" and threw the paper in the rain barrel so she would "play" with us. Can't remember getting into much trouble.

Grandma and myself would listen to "Stella Dallas" a radio Soap Opera. When we heard Grandpa's tractor coming up the drive, we would hurry and turn off the radio, as he hated for us to listen to it.

Grandma just hated to see kids blowing bubble gum. Butch and I set up a "tent" with a blanket and chairs. Butch didn't know to blow bubbles with bubble gum and me being four years older, I taught him how to blow bubbles underneath the tent. He learned how and didn't even bother Grandma.

My Aunt Zora always took us fishing. One time I caught a "huge" catfish on a cane pole and I was so excited that I jerked it out of the pond and into a nearby tree. Aunt Zora and my Aunt BB got to get it out of the tree. What Fun!

Sisters, Shirley and Patsy "Pat" live in Lubbock Texas.

Fourth Generation Remembers
Memories of good times at Grandma and Grandpa's
By Patsy Allen Sharbutt

Driving from Borger, TX to Oklahoma looking out the window, I saw so many trees, oil Wells, cows and horses and the "big" Lake Texhoma.

At Grandma's the country garden was always fun to pick and delicious, very different from grocery food in the city.

One Sunday morning, after church, I didn't change my white dress before I went outside to see what all the commotion was about. Aunt Zora was killing a chicken by "ringing" its neck off so we could cook the chicken for dinner. I turned around and fell into a puddle of black mud and my white dress was never the same. My mother was very unhappy.

On some Sunday afternoons, our Uncle Lloyd and Uncle Boyd's kids came to play at Grandma and grandpa's house. Good memories!

Fun times to remember were the digging of worms and going to the fishing tanks. Aunt zora would dig the worms and we would put the worms in the can with a stick. We also would take a stick holding them down to put on the hooks. We city girls couldn't touch those wiggly creatures!

Vacation Bible School was lots of fun also. I enjoyed the cookies and Kool-Aid and the most fun making the crafts. Of course, my Aunt Marie was in charge of crafts.

On one occasion, some of our family came to visit. Twin Boys each had a zippy monkey and brought them in to play with. One of the twins left his Zippy and my cousin; Brenda decided that Zippy monkey was "hers". When they discovered the monkeys were missing, they turned and drove back to the house. By this time, Brenda had hidden the monkey. I had a hard time deciding to let Brenda keep the monkey or give the monkey back to the little boy. My conscience was weighing heavy; so I had to give back the monkey.

It was so sad when we when back in January of, 1958, for Grandma's funeral. As we drove in town, I looked out the window and kids were out of school because we had so many family and friends that knew her. I never saw so many people and flowers.

The thing I remember the most about my Grandpa, before he died, was his days sitting in his rocking chair with all the cousins and slamming all the doors. When I came thorough, I would make an effort to close the doors very quietly and he would tell me how much he appreciated not letting the doors slam.

Good memories always remain. Our children have a lot of good memories also; homemade ice cream, fish fry's, and catching fireflies in a jar that would light up a room. Feeling free riding bicycles, three wheelers, tractors, horses, and fishing and just good old fashion country fun with their cousins.

Pat's three children Tina, Justin, Amanda and sister, Shirley's son, Brandon. Grandchildren of Velia Newton Allen.

Fourth Generation Remembers Twelve-Mile Prairie
Brenda Gardner Weatherbee

I like to remember growing up at Grandpa, Grandma, and Zora's house until I was five years old. Grandpa, Uncle Lloyd and Boyd would play the French harp, guitar and banjo; we would sing gospel and old songs. Shirley would take me the well to look at the frogs. We both still like frogs. One year my two boy cousins from California came with Monkeys they had got new. Boy did I like those monkeys so I hid them under the bed, the boys left but came back for the monkeys so I felt bad and gave them back. They still tease me about it. I spent a lot of time taking care of my younger bothers or watching the supper while Momma went to the garden. But all in all it was good most of the time. We all loved each other.

Fourth Generation Remembers Twelve-Mile prairie
Barbara Newton Kendrick

I remember making the trip from California to Durant, Oklahoma for two weeks every year during the time my Grandparents were alive. One particularly memorable event was when I was about seven or eight years old and went to the outhouse (which was extremely frightening due to the fact that I just knew I was going to fall through the hole in the seat). This time I waited and waited until it was almost too late, then decided that the pain wasn't going away, so I might as well go do my business.

Just as I sat down, I felt the most terrible pinch or stab or something equally as painful right on my bottom, and heard something moving around under me making a frightening noise-sorta like a cackle or squawk. I screamed and jumped up and ran out-without rearranging anything on my body. Of course, you guessed it. It was a chicken or rooster or whatever. Believe me; when ever I went to the outhouse after that, I checked every nook and cranny for the chicken monsters.

Fourth Generation Remembers Twelve-Mile Prairie
Betty Newton Young

My memories were of Aunt Thelma, she had all of us children to pray before we went to bed. Uncle Lloyd and Aunt Thelma had fresh milk and I didn't like fresh milk. Grandpa Newton's storm cellar had canned food and I crawled under Uncle Lloyd's barbed wire fence and cut my back.

Fifth Generation Remembers Twelve-mile prairie
By Randy Adams
Stories I Recollect
Well house Bull

Me and Ole' Bart it was between papaw' old house and his new house. We's coming across one day there was an old bull, out there and that ole' bull got to chasing me and ole' Bart. The only thing we could see was that old well house.

We ran out there and jump upon the well house and the bull circled around that old well house and he was trying to eat our shoes and everything else he could get a hold of.

He did this for a good hour or so I, reckon until papaw' came and said" boy's what are you doing on top of that well house." And we said "that bull's after us." He started laughing. I never seen an old man laugh so hard in all my life as that ole' man laughed that day.

Hay hauling

I tell about the time we went hay hauling. It was me, Barry and Uncle Melvin. We was going back into this back pasture, to pick up some hay. You remember that old 56' Chevrolet truck, boy I used to ride upon that front fender and it had a big ole' blinker up there on it and I used to hang onto it while ids' riding. Now ole' Barry he got a wild hair one time and I guess he thought he was Richard Petty or something like that. He started trucking out across that ole' oat field and as just as fast as that ole' truck would go and here I was upon that ole' truck fender trying to hang on I looked like a ole' bull rider or something and ole' Melvin in there sitting on the passengers seat he was bouncing up and down hitting his head on the roof of that old truck and he was yelling "slow down" "slow down" and ole' Barry was laughing his ole' head off and here I was out on the Fender that truck thinking its wonder if I didn't fall off and break my neck. That crazy nut!

Another time pa' paw' was paying us a nickel a bale, I was to little to be picking up that hay and such he had that old loader that you put on the side of the truck. I would set on the fender and if one of the bales got side ways that was my job to straighten it up. I think that's how Berry learned to drive was that old truck. I tell you what that old truck got used one time a year and every year we would go out there and piddle with that old truck but it never fail to start. You would be driving and look down at you feet and their would be mice and rats running all over your feet and such. And the seat there would be nothing but the springs holding it together.

Fun in the Barn

Tell you there was one other time we kind' a got into trouble a little bit we would go into the old barn and built hide outs and forts with the bales of hay. And also we built a swang and hang sticks from the rafters in the old barn. And one other time we when into the chicken house and had us an egg fight needless to say we kind' a got in trouble about that too. We didn't steal any eggs no more.

Big Black Bull

One other year Papaw bought this big ole' black Brangus bull and it kept getting out of the fences. Papaw was trying to put it in the pen. Bart and me was out by the old house and papaw' and some one else was trying to run the bull back into the gate. Papaw got on that ole' International tractor trying to round that bull up. That ole' bull got in the middle of the road and started charging Bart he was so scared and that ole' man jump off that tractor without even stopping it and got between the bull and Bart he hit the ground run past the bull and jump in front of that bull before it got Bart. I reckon' he was lucky he didn't get killed. For a short-legged old man he could run.

Papaw' could Run

We were out there behind the ole' new house we were out there in the cotton field checking to see if it was ready for harvest. We challenged papaw' to a foot race papaw' said all right when I say go, you take off. So he said one for the money two for the show three to get ready and four to go. Man he kick up tons of dirt and dust and we got half way down the field we were all tuckered' out and when we got to the house papaw' was setting at the bar drinking coffee we were a bout to die we were trying to get our air, when papaw' said" what took you boys so long. He had those little short legs you every saw but those short legs could run.

Fishing

There's some the best fishing you'd' ever seen down there in them ole' ponds. Pa' paw' had and ole' pond, a big ole' pond

There by the barn it was full of perch and you could go down there with a bare hook and catch all the perch you want. You could just set there under that ole' bois'd Arc' tree and catch fish all day long.

One time we made a little money we went to Gibsons and bought us one them Zebco 202, store bought fishing rods and ole' Pa' Paw' he went fishing with us that day. It was a pretty warm day and we had our new fandangle' fishing rods and some fishing lures, them there store bought fishing lures. We were all out there casting and throwing them lures. Now Papaw' had this 12 foot cane pole we" said you ant going a' catch any fish with ole' stick and a string." So Pa' Paw' loaded up a big ole' piece of chicken liver upon that hook and slung it out there and just sit there fishing. We wouldn't' catching nothing after about an hour we saw him stand up and started walking backwards we thought what in the world is he doing. He catches a thirteen-pound catfish. We were just setting there with our new fandangle rods not catching nothing. That ole' school-fishing well beats new day fishing anytime I reckon'.

Id' tell you fishing down there in them ole' ponds can't get any better. One day we went down to ole' man Perkins place. They said better not let him catch you down there. I don't know if he would done anything or not but we never got caught. On the way down there we got us a mason jar and we catch bait we caught them yellow grass hoppers and Barry went with me down there we caught more fish than we could bring home. That stringer was so heavy we had to get us a big long stick like them boys over there in Africa we had to carry all them fish, no telling how many pounds we had.

Ole' Bee the Milk Cow

Ole' Bee that old milk Cow I remember you could rub her on top of her head and she would butt your hand off. One day we's down there and Pa' Paw' his going to milk her. So we were gathering eggs while Pa' Pa' was milking and when we got back. We were sitting upon the fence there by the coral. Directly we heard the dogs barking I think it was bama his little white dog he came threw chasing a rabbit up underneath that ole' cow and bee kicked Pa' Paw' right square in the head it knock him down and he just got right back up I, know it hurt bad he didn't' cuss I, think I ever heard him cuss he didn't say a word. He had a big ole' hoof print up on his ole' head. Pa' Paw' he just put the milk bucket under the cow and started milking like nothing ever happens luckily it didn't knock him out.

Vacation/Summer break

I remember going down there on vacations and summer breaks. We always had a good time, Papaw' was always first one up and first one to bed. We get up and he would have breakfast all ready. He'd be drinking a cup of coffee he'd always have biscuits and gravy the way he made them biscuits he would dob some bacon grease on them that would make um' better.

Ant never seen an old man work harder in my life than that ole' man. He told us things and he showed us the proper time to pick the corn to see if it when it was ready to pick and to pick the tators. Anything you could think of he shows us how to do it. He also shows how to drive the tractor and such and he taught us all how to drive. I guess we were the only young en's out there on his place. I know he was never wrong about anything he told us.

Terrapin/Tarantula

We'd be walking down them dirt roads and he would see a Terrapin and he'd say see a Terrapin crossing the road its goin'a rain. If you see a Tarantula its going to rain and if you see a Terrapin and a Tarantula it goanna' come a flood. He said now if you see tarantula in the road ya'll don't be going around them they can jump upon your stomach and bite a whole right threw you. Now I don't believe it.

Raccoon Hunting

They would say don't go back in the woods the wolves will get you. We wanted to go hunting but they had us scared of the bottoms. One night Uncle Jimmy went with us he had his ole' coon dog's with him. And we'd wonder now if we can't go down there in the daytime. What in the world are we doing going down there at night for. We finally figured out we could go down with out being ate up.

I remember we's down there raccoon-hunting with Uncle Jimmy he'd get those ole' dogs barking and he'd' howler and he'd say "woo" "woo" and that would make them ole' dogs bark that much louder. Yes I, was just a little boy and that was some good ole' times. Luckily we didn't get killed.

Aunt Zora

Aunt Zora had and ol'e pond down there in the woods and it was full of snakes, "water moccasin" I don't guess it had any fish we 'd go down there with a 22-caliber rifle and shoot them snakes. I guess the good Lord was looking after us because we came out of there "ok".

Papaw's Long Tom Shotgun

Ol'e papaw he had his ole' shotgun he'd say now boy's that gun shoots in front and kills behind. I guess he was trying to scare us because we didn't shoot that gun for a long time. So one day we found some shells we took that ole' long tom out there in the back pasture and shot that ole' gun and he was right it shot in front and killed behind. I shot that ole' gun and it turned me a flips. It kicked me so hard I never shot that gun again. There were things we did and never got caught, we were pretty slick we never got into trouble but I think they knew what we were doing.

Song
Twelve-Mile Prairie
Written by Boyd Lynn Newton

Chorus:

Where that twelve-mile prairie stretches out of sight,
There's not a tree, not a fence post to slow the breeze at night
With our baby's arm's around us boy's there Holden us tight
And crickets sing our lullaby cause everything's all right

1st verse

Well my daddy was born there back in, 1922,
Since then it seems like he has too much work to do
Getting'n up early every morning before the rising sun
And long after sundown before his work was done

2nd verse

Well now I've worked this music cause we have paid our dues
I like to play my ole guitar while my daddy harp's the blues
We got lot of friend around us cause they like good music to
On the twelve-mile prairie we'll sing and play for you

Song
Daddy
Written by Linda Kaye Newton Holland

1st verse

My daddy was a farmer when I was a kid; He never made any money, he loved what he did.
He'd get up in the morning and go milk the cow; he'd get his old mules and go to the field and plow.
He took us to church on Sunday and taught us how to pray and
I remember the things he use to say.

Chorus

Young'ns don't forget where you come from, Gods been good to you, be proud you were raised in the country; stand up for the red white and blue
Won't hurt to get dirt on your breaches when you go the woods and pray young'ns don't forget where you come from, where I'm going, gon'na meet you there someday.

2nd Verse

I walked the fields he planted the day he past away, I thought of how I, would meet him again on that glorious day but until then,
I'll continue on working and tending to his fields hoping, I can do things the way my daddy did.

Song
Daddy's Girl
Written by Lola Newton

When I was a little girl, a growing up at home
I looked up to my daddy, and tried to do no wrong.
My daddy is an honest man; he always earned his due,
And if you ask our neighbors, they'll say the same thing to.
He'd sit out on our front porch and talk about the stars
He'd tell us bout the noises coming from the dark
And when we'd ask ott is it he would kindly say
It's just and old hoot owl my child, don't fear I'm here to stay.
Daddy's girl, that's what they call me
Daddy's girl, who could ask for more.
Daddy's girl oh how I love it
Daddy's girl forever more.
He'll take that harp in his hands
And play a freight train song
It makes me want to sing and dance and stay up all night long
Now that I've grown older though time has changed my name
My feelings for my daddy will always be the same.
He's tried to teach us right from wrong, be as good as your word.
Although the world keeps changing, his words should still be heard. It's my prayer he feels all the love and respect that I have inside my heart each time I hug his neck.
Daddy's girl, that's what they call me.
Daddy's girl, who could ask for more.
Daddy's girl, oh how I love it,
Daddy's girl forever more
Daddy's girl you know I love him
Daddy's girl forever more.

Song
Fifty Years of Loving
Written by Boyd Lynn Newton

Half a century ago in a January snow two young lovers said "I do"
Dad was back home from the war and mom was just a bright-eyed girl
And from there they watched as their family grew
When those storm clouds gathered round in each other's arms they found
Reasons to keep fighting against the wind
Sometimes it wouldn't rain a drop or the hailstorms would destroy the crop
But they always found the strength to try again.
Chorus
Cause after fifty years of livin' Lord there is fifty years of love
And fifty years of memories that they made four girls a boy a farm, a store and looking ahead there is so much more.
In this life of theirs they would never trade
Sometimes I know it was so hard all the work there on that farm
And other times life would seem so sweet
My daddy loves to work his fields and Momma's bible well that's her shield and together they make a team that can't be beat.

Poem
How Proud Am I?
Written with love by B.B. Newton and dedicated to my three stars.

You ask, how proud am I,
Oh this tear in my eye, why
It isn't because I am sad
But because I'm very, very glad.
Look up there and tell me who you see.
Those three on the end, they belong to me.
That gent there with the harp is one of the dears
He's been my husband for nigh on Fifty-Eight years
That young lady singing she's such a pearl,
Did you know that she is my little girl?
And the man with the guitar and ponytail,
In earlier days he was as thin as a rail.
Oh I'm sure, for he's my baby, my only boy
And of course, all of our pride and joy.
So I ask you, is it any wonder why,
Occasionally you see a tear slip from my eye
And slide down my check onto the floor?
As I watch with pride, the ones I ADORE.

Poem
My Other Three
Written By B.B. Newton and dedicated to the other three Love Mom.

A while back, I think a week or two ago
I told you about part of my family that I love so.
It's was about those on stage that I adore,
But did you know that there are more?
To be exact there are three
And they all mean just as much to me.
Three precious rosy cheeked little girls

With chubby little fingers and golden curls,
And smiles that would light up the darkest day
And totally steal your heart away.
I watched as into womanhood they grew,
And sighed in my heart because I knew
Some day soon some guy would come along
And my little girls would be gone
To begin a new and different life
Not as my little girls, but someone's wife.
Jolene was the first to leave the nest,
Then was followed the rest.
Joey, as we called her was not only smart
But always had the biggest heart.
Then there was carol, the last to go
Gentle, sweet Carol, I missed her so.
Kathy full of giggles and sweet charm,
Taught school, drove a truck and now works on a farm.
Oh, yes and in an office down town,
As does the other three that I think deserve a crown.

Poem
To Boyd W with Love
Written by B.B. Newton with all my love.

Fifty-six years ago today
It hasn't been so long ago it seems
I began life in a very new way
And it fulfilled all of my dreams.
I was so young. So much in love
The day I became your wife
And God was smiling from above
Because He gave you to me for life.
The days passed quickly, into years
So very fast, where did the time go?
There were laughter there were tears,
It didn't matter, we loved each other so.
The years have bought us much joy,

Four of the sweetest darling little girls,
Last of all a very precious little boy.
These set our world in a whirl.
The years have come and gone
I loved you then with all my heart,
As you know, just you and you alone,
But more now then from the start.

Poem
Where Did All The Color Go?
Written by B.B. Newton

I went outside this morning and looked all around
And found that our world had turned a dismal brown.
I observed the once green, but now naked trees
With not a leaf left to whisper in the breeze.
The many tiny humming birds that I adore
Were not to be seen at their feeders anymore.
I begin to ponder the beauty of the past year,
And to my surprise, on my cheek I felt a solitary tear.
I whispered into the air, where did all the color go?
It was so very beautiful, and I miss it so!
I remembered spring, with trees decked in there very best,
To make a safe haven for fowls of the air to make their nest.
The hillsides and valleys were lush with grass so green,
Dotted with wild flowers, a colorful sight as you've ever seen.
There were reds, yellows, and blues that seemed to be everywhere
And their fragrance floated through the fresh spring air.
Birds of all kinds darted to and fro in the dear blue sky,
It was then I know and did not wonder why all the brilliant colors had to go away
and leave in its stead such a dreary, bleak day.
Then came summer, with warm still air and the days long.
The butterflies and hollyhocks sang a summer song.
Bees buzzed busily around golden peaches on the old peach tree
The vine, heavy with clusters of red tomatoes, beckoned to me.
The sun shone down brightly with its hot shimmering rays
Spreading through the air the scent of the fresh mown hay.

Clouds came, and the dry earth opened its mouth to welcome rain, and soon the fields were ablaze with ripe, golden grain.
Then we saw the landscape change and began to go, soon there will be another to admire, I'm beginning know.
Then there was autumn, and God with paintbrush in hand
Turned the earth into a patchwork quilt to cover the land.
Mums burst into vibrant colors, yellows, gold, bronze, copper and red and the trees followed suit, changing the forest into a giant flowerbed. Squirrels scampered about, busily storing food for the winter ahead, and the birds that were so plentiful a few days ago have all fled.
They flew to the south in search of a warmer place to stay
But will return when the cold winter days have gone away.
The once lovely leaves are gradually turning brown and disappear,
Telling us for sure that fall is past and winter is near.
Winter was ushered in with a cold windy blast; we shivered when we thought about how long it would last.
But Mother Nature was not through, her beauty to show,
For we awoke one morning to find new fallen snow.
As we slept it had quietly blanketed the ground,
As the sun rose, the tree glistened everything sparkled all around
Like tiny diamonds, while the cardinal hopped about in nature's display, and the earth was dressed in grandeur, if but for a day.
For the sun would shine warmly and soon erase this work of art,
And make ready the world for a new season, a new start.
To now I do not ask "Where did all the color go?"
Because I know it was God's plan, from long, long ago.
For with each season there was new beauty to behold, Greens, reds, yellows, blues, bronze, copper and gold.
That there was a time to plant, and a time to harvest,
Times relax, a time to ponder, a time to rest. And to remember that soon will come a New Year and spring not far behind, and then color will again be here. Trees will bud, bees will hum, birds return, flowers bloom, then we for a while can say good-bye to all of winters gloom.
By B.B. Newton

The family will always remember this story of our first Christmas tree.
Told to us by Dretha Newton Goodwin.
The Christmas tree

One cool day in December, when we were kids, my sisters and I decided we were in the Christmas spirit. We would like to decorate a Christmas tree. That was something we had never done. We decided to pop corn, and string it we also found wild red berries, to string. We cut angels out of brown paper sacks, to hang, but we didn't have a Christmas tree. We decided to go into the woods to look for one. We found the perfect tree but we didn't bring the axe. We had to go back home and get the axe and hope we could find the tree again. After looking for a while we managed to find it and chopped it down. Now we had to drag it over a mile back home. We were so excited about it we forgot how tired we were. Our Mom said "children you know you can't bring that tree in the house." So I told Mom "please let us have it on the back porch, I don't think Jesus will care if we put it there." Therefore, Mom talked it over with dad, said a prayer, and decided to let us bring it in the house. It was "most exciting." We decorated the tree with the things we made and it was the most beautiful Christmas. I will never forget it. Amen

Reminiscences of my Siblings
Loyd Wayne Newton

Gathering in the company of my brother and sisters always have brought laughter to tears from the joy of their presence from the fellowship and the closeness we joke of our childhood gathering which leave us with the uncontrollable aching in our stomach from the laughter.

First I start with my special sister Janell. Describing this wonderful person is "sensitivity." Someone I could look up to "a friend for life." I could see my reflection she held the mirrors: our images of whom we are and one we can become.

Living with her and sharing the pause of destiny she cuddly me. As a baby cared for and let me, share her bed for mother was too sick to tend to me.

Janell was my first special bond with the family. She became someone who shared blood and history and dreams, common ground and the unknown adventures of the future, darkest secrets, and glassiest beads of truth.

How happy I, was to see her waiting outside school for me the day I got my first report card. She gave me my first music lesson. Upon graduating form high school, her first vacation was with aunt Ruby and uncle Melton the vacation in Florida.

She had a fair complexion with blonde hair and beautiful green eyes. Returning she was slightly darken in color. Remembering how much I missed her.

The next sister was my special sister Dretha.

She looked at you as a catastrophe view of art. Linking the threads of our experience that became interwoven. She was that one that did not like the experiences of sorrow, pain, of affliction of any kind, she was a defender, a listener, conspirator, counselor and a sharer of delights but has a heart that wishes to relieve, and vibrate celebrations. She has the ties that bind like solid steel, ties you cannot see, only feel. She will be my sister until death and will be there threw all my boring and tedious dilemmas and will tolerate what ever I throw in her path.

The next sister is my special sister Linda Kaye, she has extraordinarily strong strengthens and compassion for nurturing that I recall from my childhood memories that crave the echoes of mother. She possess that disentangle intuitive unspoken kindness.

Reminiscences of my only living brother Jim, as a child you shared my space and knew my enter soul and now possess an extra devotion for family. My wish for you is that all your wishes come true. All through our childhood we were treated as twins by mother. Where you seen one your seen the other and mother's joy was to dress us alike. Jim and I still have that special bond. Last, but not least, is my special sister Elaine, just because she is the baby of the family; she received special attention from all the family. Elaine has that unique existence of compassion. If given the opportunity to go back in time it would be with out reservation the time spent while at Twelve Mile Prairie.

Conclusion

The solitary sojourn is to listen to the music of the rain and the caress of the wind. Observing the years of my life, special gifts of grace, have nurtured. The truth is, happiness is a learned behavior and it takes the majority of us a lifetime to obtain. A loving heart and a clear conscience can allude to laughter, for this is the music of life. The only time that is truly "our time" is this time, where we are right now. Moreover, what we do with this time is ours to decide. The wonderful thing about being human is that we can choose how we act at any given moment.

I have received many time-honored gifts from life, gifts that will expand and grow in significance over all the days to come. The idiom comes with lexis first it is to the artist that paints with diverse shades of color to facilitate the visual that he has in his mind. Second it is the author that writes the words and words is what they have to paint the picture. Third it is groups that convey steps of revitalization and curative. Fourth to the family their exclusive purpose to protect and nurture the nest. Final it is that extraordinary individual that immediately responds to you and makes your day.

Upon this land, that truly God has made placed a family rooted & grounded with His grace! From the prairie to the streams and the lakes, it was Elohem! From the beginning till, the end in my mind I will always think of him! From the dawn of every new day let me come and pray! Giving Him thanks to let me stay!

Family, heirlooms lie at the heart and soul. The value is measured by the memories it sparks the sense of history it holds. Within our dreams and aspirations, we find opportunities. The incentive is realizing that it is not the one who starts the race but the one that endures until the end and finishes.

Walk with the wise the grace of God is adhesive. Life is a trust that allows a significant test for you to face, to be greater than the grace God gives you to handle. Love is the lasting heritage irresistible surge of will unique in situation.

Allowing you to look the world in the face and experience that endless silence that we will experience someday when the soul meets God forever.

References

ancestry.com/cgi-bin/
sse.dll?gsfn=goerge+Washington&gsln=Newton&gsby=1 ...

ancestry.com/cgi-bin/
sse.dll?gsfn=william+edward&gsln=Newton&gsby=1873 ...

ancestry.com/cgi-bin/
sse.dll?gsfn=Della+R+nancy&gsln=Penny&gsby=1875& ...

civilwar.nps.gov/cwass/
soldier_results.cfm?maxcount=1480&start=1461&unit ...

civilwar.npsgov/cwss/template.cfm?unitname=38th
%20Regiment%2C%2C%20Vi ...

civilwaralbum.com/washita/1842_his.htm

civilwaralbum.com/indain/mcculloch_1973.htm

civilwaralbum.com/Indian/ardmore_cem1.htm

Collin County Living Civil war Historians, Dennis Todd and Rodney Stell: Civil War re-enactment.

durantchamber.org/history.html

digital.library.okstate.edu/Chronicles/v007/v007p175.html

etext.Virginia.edu/civilwar/booker/themes.html

en.wikipedia.org/wiki/Oklahoma_Territory

familysearch.org/ENG/search/IGI/
individual_record.asp?recid=100173114015 ...

Geocities.com/CapitolHill/9145/38history.html

itd.nps.gov/cwss/personz_Detial.cfm?PER_NER=371947905311584000003

ou.edu/special/albertctr/archives/gdweb.htm

ok.gov/osfdocs/stinfo2.html

ptsi.net/user/museum/dustbowl.html

rootsweb.com/~cenfiles/va/Mecklenburg/1850/1850cena.txt

rootsweb.com/~vameckle/1about.htm

rootsweb.com/pub/usgenweb/ok/bryan/history/before.txt

Smithsonian Magazine April edition 2005 Conquering Polio by Jeffrey Kluger

va-scv.org/site/Home.html

978-0-595-61105-8
0-595-61105-2

Printed in the United States
124346LV00004B/88-96/P